Stop Anxiety Now

**End Nervousness for Good and Experience
Relief With 42 Effective Anxiety
Management Treatment Techniques.**

**Get Your Happiness Back and
Find Your Inner Peace**

Derick Howell

Your Free Gift

This book includes a free bonus booklet. All information on how you can quickly secure your free gift can be found at the end of this book. It may only be available for a limited time.

TABLE OF CONTENTS

INTRODUCTION

Psychological and mental health conditions affect so many people in society today. In this book, our main focus will be on anxiety disorders. Research shows that anxiety disorders have become prevalent among the population. They may even affect you!

In this book, we will learn about anxiety disorders, the symptoms of different anxiety disorders, and some of the ways to effectively address anxiety in your life.

Anxiety in itself is not entirely a bad thing. At times anxiety can be a lifesaver since it triggers our awareness of the potential threats to the safety or comfort of our lives. It is an evolutionary trait that is meant to protect us from danger. Normally, it works as a natural personal alarm system that motivates us to avoid threatening or dangerous situations. For instance, when you are anxious and use the energy in a positive way, you might have the extra adrenalin to meet a difficult project deadline. In normal cases like that, anxiety is supposed to be a temporary motivator; however, at times, it may exceed its normal function and take you to uncomfortable places.

When anxiety overflows and we are unable to turn off our heightened state of mind, anxiety may flood the mind with toxic thoughts and worries. This results in the body releasing excessive amounts of stress hormones. You may become scared, nervous, overwhelmed, or even physically ill due to the heightened level of stress you are in.

When this happens, you may be confused about what is happening to your body and mind. Rest assured; you are not alone! Many people suffer from anxiety, and we will help you learn about how anxiety makes you feel, and what to do to minimize the level of impact that anxiety has on your life.

This book will help clarify facts about anxiety and give you useful tools to assist you when you experience anxiety in your life. If you have an extreme anxiety condition and are worried about the impact of anxiety on your health, consider consulting a medical practitioner instead of relying on self-diagnosis and self-treatment.

CHAPTER ONE:

Everything You Need to Know About Anxiety

Stress is a natural part of life, but sometimes our bodies may not handle stress well. Sometimes stress can become anxiety. Anxiety can be a helpful, natural response to stress. It can be classified as a feeling of fear or extreme apprehension. You may be afraid of what is about to happen, or what will happen in the future. As a child, you may be fearing your first day of school. As a parent, you may be anxious about your child's first day and how they will get along without you. When you attend an interview, you may be stressed and anxious about your performance. In most cases, people become nervous about various explainable reasons. This anxiety is normal and natural, and most people can control it well enough to function successfully at home, at work, and in the community. However, some people may have extreme feelings of anxiety and have difficulty coping with it. Such feelings may interfere with your life drastically and may indicate that you have an anxiety disorder.

Anxiety Explained

Anxiety disorders are classified by The American Psychiatric Association (APA/Parekh, 2017) as one of the most common types of emotional disorders. Anxiety affects both children and adults and has no racial or gender boundaries.

As we have already learned, sometimes people feel anxious about things that have happened, are happening or are going to happen. It is normal to wonder and worry about things. It is natural to be anxious when moving to a new home, taking an exam, or interviewing for a new job. Such stress and anxiety can be unpleasant, but for most people, it can be managed. It may even motivate you to work harder. Ordinary anxiety usually comes and goes, and it does not interfere with your life very much.

On the other hand, for those with anxiety disorders, fear and worry may overcome their lives, and the intensity of the feelings can be debilitating emotionally, psychologically, and physically. If anxiety and being in a state of constant distress affects you, you may not be able to lead a normal and healthy life. Anxiety may affect your life so much that you are unable to enjoy events and activities with family, friends or colleagues. Some people are unable to attend events, go shopping, cross the street, ride an elevator, or even leave their home. Anxiety may give you a range of debilitating symptoms including panic, sweating, heart palpitations and illness.

Generally speaking, when anxiety is not treated, it gets worse over time; however, if you learn how to control and manage these feelings, you can move beyond anxiety and lead a full and normal life.

If you suffer from anxiety, it is important to know what kind of anxiety disorder is impacting your life. This knowledge will help you identify your symptoms and triggers, as well as help you understand what you need to do to manage your symptoms.

Aren't All Anxiety Disorders The Same?

There are a variety of different anxiety disorders and they are not the same, although they may seem similar. All of them render a person unable to cope with the normal and extranormal things that life throws at us. These disorders have unique characteristics. An anxiety reaction may be triggered by something specific, or it may be an ongoing underlying factor in someone's life. Depending on the type of anxiety disorder, the impact on a person's life can range from a minor ongoing issue to a complete inability to function. The severity of the disorder will vary from person to person. Depending on the severity of the symptoms, anxiety may have a profound effect on the life of the sufferer of the anxiety, and on those around them, especially loved ones. There are many anxiety disorders that have been categorized and described. Some of the most common ones are described below.

Generalized Anxiety Disorder (GAD)

People with GAD experience excessive anxiety and worry constantly about many things including their health, daily activities, and routines, social and work interactions and circumstances that may come up unexpectedly. If you have GAD, you are likely considered "a worrier" by your friends and family. You may review pending events over in your head trying to figure out all the things that could go wrong. You may be persistently nervous about everything, and you have trouble sleeping because your mind is racing with all the worries you have. You may be tense and irritable and feel fragile all the time as you try to go through everyday life.

Social Anxiety Disorder

This is a condition whereby people worry excessively about being in social situations. They may fear interacting with strangers or family because of a fear of being judged, or "saying the wrong thing" or being inappropriately dressed. There may be a fear of embarrassment. People with social anxiety tend to avoid situations such as parties, gatherings, and other events where they will have to interact with people. Such people tend to suffer from self-imposed isolation. This is also known as a social phobia, whereby you are overwhelmed by the demands of a social situation. You may constantly think about being ridiculed, among other things. Sometimes it can manifest as being afraid of being away from home or our loved ones, but most often it is associated with a fear of interacting with others.

Panic Disorder

People with panic disorder tend to suffer from episodes of intense fear and dismay which usually comes upon them suddenly. These episodes are called "panic attacks". A panic attack may occur unexpectedly and be brought on by a trigger such as an object or situation that a person may fear. This is a disorder whereby your body takes over and you experience a physical reaction as a result of the stress. You may begin hyperventilating, have heart palpitations or chest pains, become physically ill, start crying hysterically, have hot and cold flashes or experience genuine terror, among other things. Panic attacks trigger the "freeze, fight or flight" reaction in us. You may feel able to cope with a situation right up until the moment before it happens, and then be struck down by a debilitating panic attack that prevents you from continuing with the pending event. A person who has had frequent panic attacks may live in fear of planning events or trying new things. This is because they worry they may suffer from a panic attack at the last minute, or at some point during the event.

Post-Traumatic Stress Disorder (PTSD)

PTSD is an anxiety disorder that many people suffer from. Some people think PTSD only affects military personnel who have been through battle; however, it actually is a disorder that can impact anyone that has been through a major traumatic event. Not everyone who has been through traumatic events suffers from PTSD, but PTSD is always a result of experiencing significant negative events.

Although this list is by no means complete, here are some examples of events that may lead to PTSD. PTSD may affect you if you have been to war, been physically and/or sexually assaulted, suffered an accident, lost a child, been emotionally or physically abused or seen something horrific.

PTSD can cause a variety of difficulties for those who have it. There is generally a pattern of recurring invasive thoughts. These thoughts are usually a replay of all or part of the traumatic event. These thoughts may come to you when you are least expecting it, and they may make the whole world grind to a halt for you. You may also suffer from anxiety and/or depression, have difficulty sleeping, be hyper-vigilant, and be triggered easily by situations or sounds into a state of fear, panic or distress, indecision, a near-catatonic state or be unable to leave your home. You may be unable to interact at work, at home or in the community because you are unable to cope with the stressors that you face. You may be unable to go to certain places or do certain things because they remind you too much of the past trauma.

Although you "may know" or be told by others that your reaction to your current situation is disproportionate to the actual level of risk, you are unable to deescalate your reaction.

Specific Phobia

Specific phobias are rooted in an intense fear of identifiable things, situations or places. Having a phobia is more than being just scared of something. A phobia is like a fear that is so extreme that you are unable to convince yourself to move past the fear. Other people may try to convince you that "there is nothing to be afraid of", but obviously, they don't feel the same panic and terror that overcomes you when faced with the thing, place or situation. There may or may not be a genuine level of actual danger or consequence that may come about as a result of that situation. Fear of heights, flying, elevators, snakes or dogs are examples of common phobia. (In this context we are not discussing specific social phobias such as homophobia, xenophobia, or other fears related to people who are different from other people).

Illness Anxiety Disorder

This is a condition whereby a person continually lives in fear of becoming ill, or where they believe they are becoming ill or are already ill. Whenever they detect a minor change in their perceived health, they may convince themselves that it is the manifestation of a serious illness. This may lead to other behaviors, such as an obsession with thoughts of dying from illness, frequent self-examination and self-reflection about the condition of the body and how it feels and functions, self-diagnosis and treatment, and/or unusually frequent trips to the doctor or emergency room. This belief about being ill generally persists even after a doctor examines them and confirms specifically that the person is not sick. This disorder is also known as hypochondria.

Do You Have Symptoms of Anxiety?

Although there are many types of anxiety disorders, you may have noticed some similarities between them. Anxiety is unique to the personal experience of each person; however, there are some symptoms and reactions that tend to be common among sufferers. These feelings may be manageable, or they may interfere with your daily life, and impact your ability to enjoy activities.

Depending on the disorder that you have, and to what degree it affects you, you may experience a variety of emotional and physical symptoms and reactions. Emotionally you may be unable to cope with an upcoming event. You may be plagued by self-doubt, feel out of control, start crying, or be fearful or panicky. Physically you may have reactions that include or range from butterflies in the stomach to a racing heart, hot and cold surges, and even throwing up. You may feel a complete disconnection between the body and the mind.

Some common symptoms of general anxiety are:

- Difficulty falling asleep due to not being able to stop thinking about things.
- Restlessness and the sense that something is always about to happen.
- A sense of doom or apprehension about the present or the future.
- Difficulty enjoying anything because of feelings of worry and fear.
- Increased heart rate and racing palpitations that come on suddenly when thinking about something or trying to do something.

- Trouble concentrating because there are too many thoughts racing through your mind.
- Rapid breathing or hyperventilating when faced with an idea or situation.

As previously indicated, you may experience some or all of these symptoms to varying degrees of severity. There are many more extreme symptoms of anxiety including panic attacks, nightmares, and disturbing intrusive thoughts that you are unable to control. You may be completely unable to go to some places or do certain things because you are unable to control extreme symptoms. Some people may even go into a dissociative state where they are unaware of their actions or are unable to communicate and function normally.

Have You Had An Anxiety Attack?

Have you ever been faced with a situation that caused you to feel completely overwhelmed by fear, panic or distress? Did this feeling build over time or progress from mild worry to an almost panic-like state? You may have had an anxiety attack.

The outward expression of an anxiety attack can vary significantly from person to person, and the feelings, symptoms, and behaviors of the person having the attack may also vary. The symptoms of anxiety may not affect everyone the same way. The symptoms may also change over time as the disorder progresses or regresses, or the situation reaches various states of resolution.

Common symptoms are similar to general anxiety, but an anxiety attack may specifically include:

- Worry and apprehension about pending situations
- Restlessness and continued attempts to get everything done
- Obsessively ruminating about the potential outcome of everything.
- Shortness of breath and hyperventilating when thinking about the tasks ahead.

- Feeling dizzy or off-balance or overwhelmed to the point of emotional fatigue.
- Hot flashes with sweating or cold chills or both.
- Dry mouth or other physical distress such as headache or stomach illness.
- Fear of people, places or the outcome of situations.
- Distress or hypersensitivity about what is happening or might happen.

Are Anxiety Attacks And Panic Attacks The Same?

While anxiety attacks and panic attacks share some common symptoms, they are not the same. The difference is easiest to understand in terms of the time they take to develop.

An anxiety attack develops progressively and is usually brought on by an upcoming event or a situation that is evolving and has an uncertain outcome. For many people, an anxiety attack may progress from a mild concern to especially acute reactions that can't be controlled. These reactions may be so severe that the person is unable to cope with continuing participation in the event, despite their original appearance of calm or competence.

In comparison, a panic attack is a direct, acute and sudden reaction to a situation, thought or event. It does not build over time into a panic state; the panic state comes upon the individual quite suddenly. A panic attack is a physical reaction to an emotional state of extreme distress about the current or shortly pending situation. You may be dressed up and ready to go, and looking forward to something, and then suddenly, you are overcome with feelings of illness or begin hyperventilating or crying as you prepare to leave. You may not understand what you are afraid of, but you are unable to move forward due to the debilitating sudden physical manifestations of panic.

What Causes Anxiety?

There are many theories about what causes anxiety disorders. Some are more forgiving than others in the amount of blame they place on the individual with the disorder. Researchers have theorized about various causes and treatments, but no one is completely sure why some people suffer and others don't.

In the case of PTSD, most people can understand that a severely traumatizing event may cause an anxiety disorder. They understand that extreme trauma will have lasting effects upon the psyche and that these effects may manifest in symptoms and behaviors that are difficult to cope with.

For those with less obvious cause and effect type conditions, it may be difficult to explain or even understand why we have these symptoms and behaviors. Doctors are still trying to understand mental health and studies are ongoing. There are many theories, but it is generally agreed that a combination of different factors may impact a person's likelihood to develop an anxiety disorder. Some factors are genetic and include brain chemistry or inherited conditions. It is also well understood that brain injuries may cause damage to the brain in a way that makes it unable to process stress in a manageable way. Some are caused by environmental factors such as living in a dangerous place, and some are a direct result of experiences that had negative consequences on us. Researchers know that there are some areas of the brain that are responsible for controlling fear and that when those areas are impacted the person may develop anxiety disorders as a result.

In general, it is agreed that anxiety is a reaction to stressors in our lives. The role of "stress" cannot be overlooked.

Anxiety And Stress

Stress and anxiety have a direct correlation. Stress usually comes about as a result of the brain's demands about a situation. When it evaluates the situation, a decision is made to be either okay with the situation, or to be "stressed about it". If you are worried about something, and it develops into stress, that may evolve into anxiety. Stress is caused by a situation that makes you uncomfortable or worried. If the mind is unable to resolve the stress in a healthy way, it may develop into anxiety, which is a more serious expression of the emotional and physical state of extreme stress.

Anxiety and stress have many of the same emotional and physical symptoms, but for those with anxiety, they are unable to resolve the stress and stop worrying. Some people are able to deal with stressors, and some people have anxiety disorders whereby they are unable to manage stress, and it takes a toll on their emotional and physical health.

Stress and anxiety can be bad, but they can also activate our body and mind to work harder and give us the adrenalin that we may need to "power through", "get through it", or "get it done". It can also ensure that you are aware of the dangers around you and take precautions. When stress and anxiety persist in a way that interferes with your enjoyment of the activities of your life, you may have developed an anxiety disorder.

How Is Anxiety Diagnosed?

Many people know they have anxiety but are unsure if they have an actual anxiety disorder. There is no single test used to diagnose anxiety disorders. Instead, an anxiety disorder diagnosis usually requires a lengthy examination carried out by a mental health professional.

Mental health evaluations are carried out by means of conversation, question and answer, and the use of psychological questionnaires. The use of a questionnaire allows the mental health professional to rate your symptoms on a standardized scale of severity. Questions are used to evaluate depression, anger, mania, anxiety, recurring thoughts, etc. and then the patient is classified based on the responses.

Some doctors may also recommend or conduct physical exams including urine and blood tests in order to rule out any underlying health conditions that may be contributing to your symptoms.

Anxiety Combined With Other Disorders

Sometimes, we may have a very complicated mental health situation. It is quite common to have an anxiety disorder combined with other conditions such as depression.

Depression

If you have an anxiety disorder, you may also suffer from depression. Anxiety and depression both impact the ability of the mind and the body to achieve joy. The symptoms of depression may worsen when they are triggered by the symptoms of an anxiety disorder. A person may be depressed because they can't control their anxiety and feel like they can't function in society. A person may be anxious because their depression is making them afraid to interact with others who might judge them because of their condition. With both depression and anxiety, being impacted in a way that is debilitating to your ability to function may require professional help to properly address.

Chapter Summary

In this chapter, we learned that stress and anxiety is a natural response of the body when we are confronted with a challenging situation. The nervous system has a natural evolutionary response to potential danger, called "freeze, fight or flight". This is triggered when the body releases adrenaline and the stress hormone known as cortisol. Anxiety is a natural response of the body to stress; however, when the response to the stressor becomes too extreme, it may signal the presence of an anxiety disorder.

We also learned how to recognize anxiety disorders, how different anxiety disorders are defined and how they are similar and different. You may have been wondering if you have an anxiety disorder, and if so, what are the symptoms? Although each person experiences anxiety in the context of their own experience, there are many similarities in the general symptoms experienced by sufferers of anxiety disorders.

Reactions may be emotional and/or physical and can range from rapid breathing or hyperventilating, increased heart rate including palpitations, hot and cold flashes often accompanied by sweating, having invasive thoughts that can't be put aside, being constantly worried or scared about everything, and difficulty sleeping due to racing thoughts. You may even experience other physical symptoms such as being physically ill, catatonia, rashes, crying or hysterical panic.

Anxiety disorders are not yet fully understood, but the science of mental health is continuing to evolve. In some instances, there are easily explained life experiences that may lead to an anxiety disorder. In other cases, there is seemingly no explanation why some people are impacted and others aren't. A true diagnosis of a specific anxiety disorder requires collaboration with a mental health professional. If you have a mental illness that has debilitating negative impacts on your life, seek the help of a professional who can supervise your diagnosis and treatment.

If you are now comfortable with your general understanding of anxiety disorders and are not sure about obtaining professional intervention at this time, you may find the information and tools that follow to be valuable assets to you as you work to manage the anxiety in your life.

In the chapters that follow you will learn a variety of different techniques you can use to deal with anxiety

CHAPTER TWO:

How To Enjoy The Present By Using Mindfulness To Minimize Anxiety

It has been shown that practicing mindfulness can help reduce the symptoms of anxiety. In this chapter, you will learn how mindfulness is defined, how anxiety is influenced by the human consciousness, how the study and practice of mindfulness have evolved, and how you can use it to manage anxiety in your life.

What Is Mindfulness?

The practice of modern mindfulness is rooted in ancient Buddhist traditions. Mindfulness requires an individual to be present in the moment and to cast aside the thoughts that distract the mind from achieving the objective that is sought at that time.

Mindfulness is a state of non-judgemental awareness of ourselves and others. Let's review this very important concept again.

Mindfulness is based on acceptance and awareness of yourself. You must foster awareness of your inner experiences, thoughts, beliefs, and processes. This awareness and consideration must be accomplished without judgment. Depending on what you have experienced in your life, you will have different things to consider.

The Role Of Human Consciousness

You may be wondering, how does mindfulness work? In order to truly understand mindfulness, we need to consider the theories related to the state of human consciousness. A keen understanding of the state of consciousness is required to understand how mindfulness contributes to better overall mental health, and specifically in the management of anxiety disorders.

The "domains of human consciousness" have been discussed, theorized upon, and judged since humans began wondering about what makes themselves think and act the way they do. The current thoughts on the domains of consciousness (Henriques, 2015) include three main areas:

Experimental domain: This is sometimes referred to as the theatre of consciousness. This part is activated and deactivated by our state of being asleep or awake. This domain is based on personal experience. It is the domain that evaluates the facts of what is actually happening or being considered at that time.

Private self: This is the part of your consciousness that provides the ongoing narrative about what is happening to you. It may be evaluating the situation through the lenses of your personal experience or worldview.

Persona: This is the side of you that you show others. Your persona is what you consciously display to others as a means to express yourself with actions and words.

The consciousness may have additional filters that allow varying degrees of consideration by our consciousness about the situation at hand. For example, each domain of consciousness is influenced by the brain's ability to ignore some things and focus on others. We may do it intentionally or unintentionally. We may give emphasis to one fact over another, or one potential outcome over another. We may think obsessively about one potential outcome when other outcomes are just as likely. Similarly, we may deliberately ignore or suppress certain things in an effort to "get over them". These filters shield the mind from the full picture. Some filters are intended to protect the private self from the public persona. For example, you may not be comfortable being alone, so in a public place, you may focus on your cell phone instead of interacting with others around you or just peacefully observing and experiencing where you are at that moment in time. Similarly, you may tell people that you're fine when really you are very anxious about something that is about to happen. These are ways that human consciousness tries to protect us from the things that give us anxiety.

One of the things about the human domains of consciousness is that they tend to try to protect us. When the subconscious is aware of trauma, it may protect us by putting up filters in the form of blockages in our memories so that we are not regularly confronted by our negative experiences. When you forcibly (whether consciously or unconsciously) block traumatic memories or are ingenuine about how your life makes you feel, your system may become unstable and negatively impacted by anxiety and stress. Due to the instability, you may be unable to cope with the things in your environment that trigger those memories or feelings. These triggers may be events, places or people that remind you of trauma.

Controlling Your Personal Narrative With Mindfulness

You may be in a state of perpetual self-evaluation and self-judgment. People with anxiety disorders often are. Now that you understand the role of the human consciousness in dictating how we think about the world around us and our place in it, imagine considering all that without the self-judgment! That is what mindfulness allows you to do.

When we expose ourselves to a full spectrum of thoughts about our reality, such that the thoughts are not filtered by denial, self-criticism, and self-judgment, we have a better, truer understanding of self and others. This understanding can help us to react to things in a way that is not influenced by our negative beliefs about ourselves or the situations we may be in or are anticipating. This is why mindfulness is so helpful in handling anxiety.

The Power Of Mindfulness

Mindfulness techniques have been used to treat a variety of anxiety disorders including generalized anxiety and PTSD, as well as related conditions such as depression and obsessive-compulsive disorder (OCD).

As early as 1979, programs such as *"Mindfulness-Based Stress Reduction"* at the University of Massachusetts Medical School were established to pursue the study and practice of mindfulness. The creator of this program, Jon Kabat-Zinn, built upon his studies of Zen Buddhism and yoga, to develop a concept about mindfulness that could be taught to others. He wrote the book *"Full Catastrophe Living"* which advocated awareness on a moment to moment basis and the consideration of things we would usually ignore or discard (Wiki, 2020; Henriques, 2015). This concept has been adopted by many medical centers and mental health practitioners to assist patients to cope with anxiety and other conditions.

The reason why Buddhist teachings are often used as a base for understanding mindfulness is because of the profound belief in the inevitable suffering of life. If suffering is inescapable, then there is no need to escape it. It needs only to become part of the full landscape of our life. Trying to banish negative thoughts creates an imbalance in us that leads to negative consequences. Being aware of the totality of life, and the balance of good and bad allows us to more easily cope with the things that unsettle us, as we are aware of them without judgment of ourselves.

In 2012, mindfulness gained further public acclaim when Tim Ryan published *"A Mindful Nation"* and was subsequently given a large grant to teach mindfulness in schools. Other noted specialists, including Richard Davidson, an accomplished neuroscientist, and the interpersonal neurobiology community used mindfulness to better understand psychodynamic perspectives, emotions and how to optimize the function of the brain. (Henriques, 2015)

Mindfulness is often expanded to include meditation, which is the ancient form of attaining total awareness and peace through the practice of sitting still, clearing your mind, and coming into a state of complete oneness with the universe. We will go further into meditation in Chapter 9.

Chapter Summary

In this chapter, you learned about mindfulness and how human consciousness works to filter our thoughts, reactions, and behaviors in the world around us.

Mindfulness is based on being aware of and considering yourself and your experiences without judgment. It can be further expanded to gain an understanding and acceptance of the situations that you are in or about to face. Being aware of and focused on what you need to do in this moment prevents you from ruminating upon what might happen later. When you practice mindfulness, you can counteract anxiety because you are considering or doing only what needs to be done in the present moment.

If you experience anxiety in any form, you may achieve great success using mindfulness. You may be afraid of the future and what may happen in your life. Consider how mindfulness can be used to focus you on what you need to do at this moment in time. Mindfulness involves paying attention to the specifics of your daily life and all the things that you usually rush through or take for granted. Focusing on being mindful of your present makes your mind unavailable to worry about what is making you anxious.

Mindfulness can be practiced consciously throughout your daily activities. It can also be practiced through meditation, which forces you to stop everything and take time to be present and aware of the totality of existence, instead of our small part in it.

In the next chapter, we will learn about what happens and what to do when anxiety attacks...

CHAPTER THREE:

What To Do When Anxiety Attacks

Anxiety and panic are real reactions that real people have to the situations around them. They may not want to feel this way but have no control over how their body reacts to the stressors in their lives. We know that the physical symptoms of anxiety may include unpleasant physical sensations and impacts upon our emotional and physical wellbeing. These sensations of doom, overwhelming inability to cope, dread, nervousness, physical illness, and emotional dismay are all real symptoms that people with anxiety strive to cope with.

Typical Anxiety Indicators

There are three predictable types of reactions that people going through anxiety may experience. Let's review each of them.

Physically Heightened State That Is Similar To Terror And Panic

This is a state of the body that is characterized by heart palpitations, shortness of breath, muscular tension, crying or hysteria and even physical illness. This happens when the body releases the stress hormones adrenaline and cortisol. As we discussed before, this is often referred to as a panic attack and is usually an immediate reaction to a specific trigger or stressor. An ongoing state of heightened anxiety that persists can have serious health consequences and has been known to lead to heart attacks and elevated blood pressure.

A "Wired" Feeling Of Tension That Is Associated With Being "Stressed Out"

Many people with generalized anxiety disorder experience the feeling of tension, stress, and dread in reaction to or anticipation of current or future activities. This can be a cycle of self-perpetuating worry that inevitably leads to increasing levels of stress as the body anticipates a resolution. When the body is constantly on edge, persistent restlessness, agitation and worry can have negative impacts on your overall health.

The Mental Anguish Of Rumination

When your brain won't stop thinking distressing thoughts, and you are routinely plagued by reruns of previous events, or anticipated scenarios, it can impact our ability to think positively and to take action. Rumination can also be associated with depression and dissociative behavior because the individual recedes into a reflective, contemplative, or worrying state that may last for long periods of time. It may cause persistent nausea and tension, or a sense of suffocating under the weight of the things you are thinking about. The ruminations may persist when we are trying to do other things, resulting in problems with concentration, and an inability to interact successfully with others.

Understand Why Anxiety Happens To You

Understanding why anxiety happens to you is often referred to as recognizing your triggers. There is usually a direct correlation between a specific stressor and the reaction of anxiety. For example, you may have been attacked by a dog when you were young. Ever since then, you have a terrible fear of dogs, and the idea of going to a park may terrify you to the point where you are unable to enjoy taking your children out in nature. An invitation to a new friend's house who has a dog may cause you to get progressively more and more anxious until right before the event, you have a panic attack and are not able to attend. Because you don't want to be judged for your fear, phobia or anxiety, you might tell them you are sick with the flu. Then you may have further anxiety because you disappointed yourself by not being able to go, and you have lied to a new friend.

A lot of anxiety revolves around the question of "what if". Often, if you are able to effectively predict the specifics of a situation, you have no reason to fear it. That is why a lot of people with anxiety disorders prefer reliable routines where things are predictable, and there is little variation. This allows for less possibility of the unknown impacting your life.

Knowing what your stressors are can help you to organize your life such that you have fewer stressors and more predictability with situations you know will trigger your anxiety. For example, you might rather miss the event than risk being judged by your new friend. However, if you tell your new friend that you are terrified of dogs and you are not sure if you can come to their house, they may just surprise you by saying, "no problem, my neighbor sometimes dog sits for us, I'll ask them if the dogs can hang out over there for the night, really, it will be less chaos in the house anyway."

Understanding why anxiety happens is the first step to managing your symptoms and finding ways to manage your stressors so they don't have such a negative impact on your life.

Fear is one of the most common reasons why symptoms of anxiety, including panic attacks, may be perpetuating a cycle of negative impacts on your emotional and physical health. If you can tell yourself that your anxiety is a normal response to a perceived threat and that you are likely "overreacting", that can be a useful tool, allowing you to talk yourself into other calming behaviors and thoughts.

Remember It Will Pass

No matter how severe your reaction to stress is, even when it is a serious panic attack, it is helpful to remember that it will pass. It may be hard to understand that when you are in the middle of a high anxiety state. No matter how "jacked up" or "obsessed" or "panicky" you feel, there is a point where another physical or emotional reaction will take over. Tell yourself, "this will pass, this will pass", and practice some techniques of managing your symptoms. The sooner you do this, the sooner the intensity of your anxiety will decrease.

Techniques For Managing Panic, Feeling Wired and Excessive Rumination

Take Care Of Your Body

It may seem like common sense, but we often forget to take care of ourselves, which can impact our ability to handle stress. This can include not eating properly, not sleeping properly and not getting any exercise. When the body is deficient in nutrients and energy, it is not capable of handling stressors in a healthy way. Some people believe that a diet that is low in caffeine, sugar and alcohol results in the body and mind being more resilient to stress and a decrease in the symptoms of anxiety. We will talk more in a later chapter about how diet and self-care routines can enhance your ability to cope with anxiety and make your reactions to stress more reasonable.

Use Deep Breathing

People often say, "just breathe", and they are right. Sometimes when anxiety is heightened, we start breathing in short jagged bursts, and may even hyperventilate. This reduces the available oxygen to the blood and brain and compounds the effects of anxiety as the state of physical distress elevates.

When you stop and take long deep breaths, slowly and deliberately, it calms the body and mind and makes us more able to attend to the situation at hand with calm and clarity. Some people call this diaphragmatic breathing or belly breathing. It is characterized by taking air slowly into your lungs and letting your belly expand with air instead of your chest, and then letting the air out slowly as you allow your belly to deflate. You can also do a version where you expand your belly first, and then your chest, and then breathe out slowly in the reverse order.

Some people swear by sessions of deep breathing, done lying down in a quiet undisturbed environment. This is, of course, the optimal practice of deep breathing for therapy. However, don't underestimate the powerful calming effect of a few deep breaths anytime you are waiting for something or feel your level of anxiety rising.

Mindful Awareness

As you learned previously, there are many benefits to a state of mindful awareness, also called mindfulness. When you are overcome with feelings of heightened anxiety or are caught in a cycle of rumination, use mindfulness to reorient you to the specifics of the present.

What can be observed at that moment? What are you doing that needs your full attention? If you want to do a full exercise, you would still your body and close your eyes. Consider how your body feels, concentrate on how you feel when you breathe, and try to take inventory of your physical sensations. Then, with your eyes still closed, shift your attention away from yourself and become aware of the sounds and smells around you, and what is happening around you. This practice is a tool that can help you to move beyond your feelings of distress because you have to deliberately silence those thoughts in order to become aware of what is around you.

Distract Yourself

Another way to be present in the moment, and effectively put anxious thoughts at bay is the time-honored tradition of distracting yourself. When you are having feelings of intense anxiety or are caught in a cycle of overthinking and rumination, it can be hard to focus on anything but your anxiety, and this can just intensify the symptoms.

It can be extremely useful to choose an activity and concentrate on doing that instead. This is especially useful if the activity requires concentration or movement. It can be hard to focus on anything other than how you're feeling during an anxiety attack and this can intensify symptoms.

If you can get your mind to focus on something else, there is less room for the anxiety in your active reality, and you may experience a significant decrease in the severity of your symptoms. There are many activities that may help. For example, listening to an audiobook, playing a musical instrument, loading wood, doing laundry, gardening or running an errand. It can sometimes be a benefit to select a chore so that you can feel good about getting something productive done. If you use a personal reward distraction, like reading or listening to a book, or singing along to some favorite music, congratulate yourself on making quality personal time for yourself.

Walk Around A Bit

You might feel as if staying in one safe contained space is best for you when you are feeling anxious. Although this can be comforting because it is predictable, it can allow you to sink further into a cycle of anxiety or other negative feelings. Like with choosing a distraction, walking around a bit can be an effective way to change your state of mind. It will help to burn off some of the adrenaline and get your blood moving, which will assist to clear your mind. Staying in one spot for too long may cause our body to stiffen and even cramp up, causing us additional physical distress. We may not realize it until we get up, so get up often and "stretch your legs" as they say. This might be the last thing you want to do when you're feeling panicky but it will help you get out of the state of mind you were in.

Release Some Tension

When the body is stressed and anxious, it often reacts by becoming tense, and we may develop pain or stiffness related to immobility and/or tension. Releasing tension is effectively done by deliberately physically changing the state of your body. If your body and mind are currently feeling bad because you are holding onto stress or anxiety, make efforts to release this tension. This can be done by breathing deeply and then exhaling all the air in a "whoosh", imaging your tension leaving your body on the breath you expel.

One of the best and most effective ways to release tension is through stretching and exercise. This forces the body into a new position and gets blood and oxygen moving through the body and brain. This movement can change your perspective and make you feel less muscular stiffness. As you stretch, your body will reward you with happy hormones like endorphins, instead of negative hormones like adrenaline and cortisol.

Summary

In this chapter you learned about typical anxiety indicators such as a physically heightened state similar to terror, being "wired" or "stressed out", and the anguish of persistent rumination. Being plagued by the constant worry of "what if" can be exhausting both emotionally and physically. Understanding why you have these reactions to anxiety is critical and being able to identify your triggers is key to improving your mental health.

You also learned some effective techniques for managing these symptoms of stress. Some of the most effective ones are taking care of your body, using deep breathing and distracting yourself to name a few.

In the next chapter, you will learn more about how to handle tension, stress, and dread...

CHAPTER FOUR:

What to Do When There's Tension, Stress, and Dread

As we have already learned, anxiety disorders can manifest in a variety of negative ways, ranging from extreme panic and anxiety attacks to a sense of perpetual tension, stress, and dread.

In order to handle your emotional and physical reactions to the stressors in your life, you must recognize your triggers and symptoms when you are faced with them. Sensations of ongoing tension and dread are managed differently than acute reactions such as panic attacks. Some of the techniques for addressing symptoms are similar because these techniques are so effective for a variety of conditions. For example, deep breathing and mindfulness are effective ways to calm and reorient yourself.

Perpetual tension and dread may be a result of the continual narrative in our minds that recycles worry and causes us to think constantly about terrible things that might happen as a result of our decisions or actions.

Don't Listen To Your Own Negative Feedback

Sometimes you may be filled with dread and feelings of tension because you are convinced of your own inadequacy or inability to cope with potential events. Because the negative voice in our head tends to be loud, persistent and domineering, it can be easy to focus on what it is saying. It is important to realize that you can change the narrative in your mind by consciously telling yourself to put aside the negative feedback and make room for the positive feedback about yourself or your situation. Tell yourself something like, "yes, yes, I know it could all go wrong, but what would it look like if it was going well", or "we've been over this before and there are other more positive ways to look at this". Envision that positive outcome and focus on letting that make you feel good.

This is similar to the idea of not believing the lies your mind tells you. The mind may lie to us to trick us into staying mentally in one place and obsessing about something. It may be telling you that you need to use all your energy worrying about a certain outcome, or that you will never get all the things done that you need to. You can choose to not believe what your mind is trying to convince you of. Don't be afraid to say to yourself and your negative thoughts, "I don't believe you. You sound really convincing, but I don't buy it. I have other options."

When Worry Calls To You, Don't Listen

When our mind and body are in a state of perpetual worry, it can be an automatic reaction to evaluate every situation or plan with a mindset of anxiety or doom. Perpetual worry and a sense of impending doom may manifest as hypervigilance in some people. This is when someone is fixated on making sure everything is safe and okay and going precisely as intended.

A state of continual focus on our fearful state can be hard to escape. This is especially true if we are busy, with many things on the go, and thus, we may feel that we have lots of things to "worry about". There may be a voice in our head that prompts us to look for something to worry about, especially if we have a free moment. This "voice of worry" is hard to turn off, and it is easy to let it dominate the theatre of our consciousness. Once you recognize that voice, however, it is easier to make choices about whether you will listen, or how much time or energy you will devote to its concerns.

When worry comes calling, tell it that you're busy actually doing something useful. Then focus on or do something positive. It may be as simple as focusing on all the things that went right today or doing something to occupy your mind with other thoughts. When you feel your body tensing up with stress, take a moment to relax your body and mind with a deep breathing exercise or a good stretch.

Make A List And Then Either Act On It Or Ignore It

This may sound like an odd strategy, but it is a way to give body and form to concerns which may be clouding your perspective and making you anxious. You may not even realize why you feel so tense, stressed out or filled with dread. Take the time to sit down and make a list of all the things that are nagging at your mind and giving you distress. Seeing your worries in a tangible form may have several benefits, including giving clarity to the reasons why you are in distress.

Seeing a list of your issues allows solutions to present themselves, which then puts your mind and body at ease. You may not realize how worried you were about getting the kids to camp until you wrote it down, which made you remember that your neighbor had already offered to take your kids with hers. This allows the identification, legitimization, and resolution of one of the things that was giving you anxiety. Add a column to the list that itemizes the ways you have planned for the item to go well, and check things off your list as you identify resolution.

Sometimes you may not have an obvious solution to all the things on the list. Sometimes the things on the list may not even make sense. They may not be anything you have any control over. That's okay! Making a list of the things that you are anxious about allows you to give them deliberate time and space in your theater of consciousness. You can choose to come back to the list or to put it aside and ignore it. This allows you to empty your mind of the worries since you can always refer to the list if you really want to or need to. Once you have the list, you must then make a conscious choice to put the list and its contents aside and move your attention to other things. These should be things that have a positive impact on you.

Focus On Fun For A While

This concept is based on the old expression that "laughter is the best medicine". When our mind is obsessed with anxiety, feelings of tension, stress, and dread, we rarely make time for or accept the potential for fun in our lives. After all, it is hard to have fun when you are overcome with worry, stress or dread! We may ignore opportunities for fun because we don't feel we deserve it. We may even feel guilty for enjoying something because we have not overcome the barriers to resolving the other issues we face.

Doing an activity that causes us to smile or laugh or play removes us from the state of worry and dread and fills us with happy hormones such as endorphins. When we are consumed with anxiety, it may be challenging to create that opportunity for fun in our lives. Take the time to play a game, go to the park with a ball or a camera, watch a funny show or listen to a funny book, play with a child or do something impulsive that you used to enjoy back when life seemed easier. If you can get yourself to laugh and lose yourself in some fun, your feelings of dread will be minimized or eliminated. We will talk more about embracing joy in Chapter 7.

Chapter Summary

At times, we are unduly affected by tension, stress, and dread. We may experience regular intervals of persistent anxiety and have difficulty moving beyond those feelings to function effectively.

In this chapter, you learned that we can make choices about what to focus on and take active steps to control our thoughts. Some of these useful techniques include not listening to your own negative feedback, not listening when worry calls to you, making a list and then either acting on it or ignoring it and focusing on fun for a while. Using these techniques gives you an opportunity to recognize what is causing you to focus on your stress and anxiety, and then put them aside in favor of more opportunities for positive outcomes.

In the next chapter, you will learn about overcoming excessive worry and thinking...

CHAPTER FIVE:

Overcoming Excessive Worry and Overthinking

In this chapter, we are going to focus more on the behavior of rumination and overthinking that keeps us in a constant state of worry.

Rumination, also called "brooding" or "overthinking" is a state of perpetual consideration of the challenges we face, or the things we have been through, or the potential outcome of future situations. It is considered a cyclical self-perpetuating behavior that can be difficult to interrupt. Like any object in motion, it is easy to keep in motion, but when it stops, it is harder to get going again. That is why interrupting the pattern of overthinking is critical to overcoming this symptom of anxiety.

Realize You're Doing It

The first step to overcoming excessive worry and overthinking is to realize and admit to yourself that you are doing it. This may not be easy, because no one wants to admit they have a debilitating condition that causes them to think obsessively about things to the point that they have no room for happiness, joy or positive thoughts. Once you realize that you are exhibiting this negative and destructive behavior, you can take action to overcome it.

Switch It Off

Once you realize you are caught in a cycle of perpetual worry, it can be hard to just "switch it off". Some people are able to just tell themselves not to worry, and their mind moves on to other things. For those with the tendency to worry obsessively about things, they may need to use deliberate exercises to assist them.

Some therapists use a method of extracting, compartmentalizing and then shelving or releasing the things that are causing our anxiety. This requires a conscious awareness of what is causing our distress. This is where that list might come in handy again! This technique requires you to close your eyes and focus on a box that is open and empty. Then you itemize an item that you are anxious about and mentally put it in the box, put a lid on it, then place it on a shelf in your mind. Tell yourself that those boxes are there for you to reference if you need them, but that you don't need them right now. The result can be a mind that is clear and uncluttered.

If you want to practice this technique in a more literal tangible way, you can expand on the use of your list. Get slips of paper and write one worry down on each piece of paper, and then put them all in a box or bag. There are various things you can do with the box or bag, including put it on a shelf, burn it or put it in the recycling to be repurposed into something new. When you acknowledge the things that you are worrying excessively about and take action to put them away, you are able to "switch it off" because you have given it meaning and a place that is external to your own mind.

Interrupt Your Thoughts

When you find yourself caught in a cycle of excessive worry and overthinking, you must make a persistent effort to interrupt those thoughts as soon as you become conscious of them. If you notice you have been thinking intently about one of your concerns, tell yourself firmly, "stop that, you're overthinking again, move along", and then consciously choose a different thing to think about, preferably something tangible to your present situation. This brings you back to the practice of mindfulness and being present for the activity we are supposed to be paying attention to. It may take hundreds of interruptions per day, but if you are consistent, you can break the pattern of your mind sinking into overthinking, just by consciously interrupting and redirecting your thoughts.

Designate Official Worrying Time

Much of the time, the things we worry about are tangible and have to be resolved at some point. If we just let our mind obsess about all of it at once, and it does this all the time, we can be overwhelmed and suffer the negative impacts of anxiety. By designating a time for worries to be recognized and processed, the mind can rest easier knowing that the issues will be addressed and that it doesn't have to constantly bug you for resolution.

Choose a time that you will dedicate to processing through your current concerns. Decide in advance how long you will spend on this activity so that you are not drawn into a long unproductive state of overthinking and worry. Carefully and thoroughly go through one or all of your worries, making a list if you want to. Identify the things that can be acted upon in the short term, make a list of those and resolve to accomplish them at a particular time. Set a time when you will revisit these worries and determine the status of the items of concern. Faithfully review the items at the designated time. This way, when persistent worry starts to creep in, you can tell it, "Hey, I already worried about you, and you're scheduled again for later, now go away".

You can take this philosophy one step further by following the practice of "only worry once". Once you have gone through the worries and given them voice and form, put them aside and move onto other things.

The extension of this is to plan instead of worry. When you identify your worries and then make a plan to resolve them and act on that plan, there is no need for the mind to obsess about them, because the outcome is determined and there is nothing left to worry about.

Go Out Into The Community

Sometimes a change of scene can make us "forget about our worries". This can be as simple as going for a walk in your community or traveling to a different town or country. Seeing how other people live and interacting with others may give us a useful perspective on the scope of our problems or help us forget our own worries for a while. Just being exposed to new input may be enough to get us out of the mental rut that rumination puts us in. If you can find something to take your mind off your worries, you may find that you are able to enjoy the things that you have been too anxious to notice.

Switch Gears

When your mind is clouded with worry and you are overthinking every situation and potential scenario, it can be useful to confuse the senses by switching gears from a state of mental fixation to a state of physical activity. This can help to shock your system into getting into a different frame of mind, one that is not obsessed with the worries you have. The transition from mental activity to physical activity may also trick the system into focussing on the needs of the body instead of the mind, providing a welcome distraction. Depending on the level of activity you engage in, you may get the added benefits of better health.

Shocking the senses interrupts the flow of negative thoughts, which can help to shut them off, or redirect them. For example, splashing cold water on your face may interrupt symptoms of hot flashes brought on by anxiety. You may take a moment to say to yourself, "wow, that's refreshing", and feel a moment of comfort and respite.

Summary

In this chapter we learned how to move beyond overthinking and excessive worry. The most important step is to realize that you are doing it. If you can identify the behavior when it happens, this awareness gives you the opportunity to stop the behavior. Some people may be able to just switch it off by saying, "now is not the time or place for overthinking this". Others may have success with visualizing the thoughts going into boxes that are arranged on an imaginary shelf, only to be accessed when we want them. Some may go even further and write these thoughts down and put them in an actual box on a shelf or take the symbolic action of burning them. Sometimes, if we designate time to address our worries and plan for their resolution, the mind will consider that enough effort spent, and restrict its worrying to that designated worry time. It can also be useful to get a change of scene by going out into the community and being exposed to other things and people to give us either perspective on our situation, or as a distraction from it. Similarly, a switch from a mentally involved state to a physically active state of the body may be enough to shock the body into releasing excessive worry and stop overthinking.

In the next chapter, you will learn how you can turn your nervousness and anxiety into excitement...

CHAPTER SIX:

Turning Nervousness and Anxiety into Excitement

We all experience emotions differently. There are so many kinds of emotions and we all go through a range of emotions in our lives. These emotions are typically generated as a response to stimuli in our environment and the expectations that we have of ourselves.

Many emotions like happiness, amusement, contentment, and love are positive and make our lives fulfilling and enjoyable. Excitement is another positive emotion. A positive emotional state can come from our own approach to life, or as a reaction to the good things that we experience. Negative emotions such as fear, nervousness, anxiety, and anger all have detrimental effects on our psychological and physical health. Negative emotional responses can come upon us as a result of fear and doubt in ourselves or as a result of things that happen to us. Nervousness and anxiety are negative emotions that hold us back from fully engaging with the opportunities in our lives.

Sometimes, we need to take time to honor emotions that put us in a negative, depressed or somewhat anxious state of mind. For example, the grief of bereavement may lead to crying and sadness, and that's okay. Give those emotions the time and energy they need. That is a positive choice. At the point that these emotions and energy drain begin to have an overwhelmingly negative impact on your life, it is time to redirect yourself into more positive expressions of your grief and lost love.

If you are experiencing nervousness and anxiety, those negative emotions may be dragging you down and making it hard to function effectively. What if you could take your nervousness and anxiety and focus all that emotional and physical energy into something positive like excitement? This is possible because the manifestations of nervousness and excitement are similar in many ways. For example, butterflies in the stomach, or feeling on edge and jittery. These signals from our body can be a positive form of energy that propels us towards completing our goal. However, when these physical expressions of nervousness build to a point of extreme anxiety, it can be debilitating.

Before that nervousness builds, try to redirect that energy into a positive outcome, like excitement.

Identify The Root Cause Of Your Anxiety

It is undeniable that people are different and so is our reaction to things. It is important for you to know that the expression of nervousness in different people can be from a variety of causes. The degree to which that nervousness turns into debilitating anxiety can depend on the intensity of exposure to the cause of the anxiety.

People have many fears about themselves and their interactions with others in the home, the workplace, and the community. Fear of failure or embarrassment, or a fear of not belonging are common. Fear is considered one of the major causes of anxiety. There are many times that you will fail to reach your full potential simply because you fear the unknown and are not able to follow through on your desired plan. So many people are inconsiderate and say, "well, you should just get over it". That may be easy for others to say, but they probably don't understand how real the feelings are for you, and how much they impact your ability to function effectively. As insensitive as their statement may have been, there is some value in finding ways to move beyond your fears and accomplish your goals, whatever they are. In order to do that, and before you can devise a lasting solution, it is important to fully understand the causes of the fear you face and eventually develop tools that help you to recognize the onset of symptoms, and redirect them into other more positive emotions.

Nervousness may also be as a result of a medical condition that you inherited. Genetic conditions and inherited traits are commonly passed down through DNA, from one generation to another. Perhaps your mother was considered a jittery woman with a lot of nervous energy. Perhaps you are also this way. Likely, you both have chemical imbalances that cause surges of adrenalin in you and make you restless and nervous as a response to stimuli in your environment. Just because she was that way doesn't mean that you have to accept this as "your lot in life". It just means that she didn't have the necessary tools to understand and treat her condition. It doesn't have to be the same for you. You don't have to accept that it is something you can't influence, manage or control. If you understand what initiates the nervous behavior, you can devise ways to manage it.

In some cases, such conditions and others may require medication and the collaboration of a psychological care provider. That's okay, and you will learn about working with a therapist in a later chapter. There are other cases where these outward symptoms of nervousness are the result of legitimate medical conditions that have nothing to do with anxiety or emotional distress. Other causes of nervous, jittery behavior may be the result of neurological medical conditions, brain injury or other physical disabilities. These conditions all require medical intervention and treatment. Other causes may include exposure to toxic substances or the use of illicit drugs like methamphetamines.

Other times, the outward expression of nervous tension and anxious behaviors may actually be the result of a positive emotion such as excitement. In these situations, the anticipation of the outcome causes jittery, on edge, hyper-focused behavior with emotional bursts and exclamations. This happens when people are focussed on watching a competitive sports game like football or hockey. Maybe your team is almost winning. Maybe this game is a "do-or-die" situation in that they might be eliminated from a championship series. Similarly, the movie or TV series might be so suspenseful that you can barely contain yourself to find out how it ends? Maybe you are waiting for someone at the airport that you haven't seen in a long time, and you are acting jittery and nervous. These are all positive expressions of excitement.

Developing a strong sense of self-awareness can help us recognize how our behaviors express our feelings. Since we understand both nervousness and excitement, and how they share many of the same physical and emotional characteristics, we can use that information to our advantage. Nervous energy may be unavoidable, but what if we could use our understanding to help direct the energy from negative nervousness to positive excitement? It is possible!

To accomplish this, try to be self-aware and understand the underlying causes of the anxieties you are trying to deal with. Since each person is different, complete your own self-assessment to determine what behaviors you express in different situations, and how close the line is between nervousness leading to anxiety, and the expression of nervous excitement.

Find Out What Triggers Initiate Your Anxiety Reaction

After developing an understanding of the ways in which your mind and body express anxiety, you are better positioned to examine what triggers this behavior. Being able to identify the causes of the nervous and anxious behaviors you may have allows you to identify what things in your environment are a catalyst for the onset of these physical responses. Understanding what causes the anxiety to dominate your mind and body is not always easy. It requires an honest effort to self-assess and observe the world around you to really understand how you feel when things happen. The specific things that trigger anxiety and anxious behavior vary from people to people, but there is a lot of common ground. It may be helpful to start with trying to understand your triggers from a broad perspective and then from a specific perspective.

For instance, students experience varying degrees of stress related to final exams. Some people handle stress with grace and calm while others suffer from anxiety and depression. They may be equally smart and have studied for the same amount of time. Why does one person become nervous and sick with anxiety? No one is really sure, but those that experience acute anxiety in some situations often have an underlying fear of failure. Also, the students may have a different expectation of the consequence of the outcome of the exams. Imagine that in your case, the results will determine whether or not you qualify for a scholarship for college. If you have other means of paying for college, then the loss of the scholarship may not cause too much anxiety for you. On the other hand, if you will not be able to go to college without winning the scholarship, the thought of not getting a good enough grade may cause debilitating anxiety. Such a dire consequence of failure may result in an inability for you to settle your mind until the results are finally released. In this case, it could be said that the exam itself is the cause of the nervousness and anxiety, but in fact, it is the fear of failure that is the root cause. Qualifying for a scholarship for college is not the cause of the nervousness, it is merely an instrument for the fear of failure resulting in a negative impact on personal or family income.

This person may have a similar emotional and physical reaction every time they are faced with a task that may have a high impact on their quality of life or basic survival needs. After all, don't forget, anxiety is an evolved trait, a characteristic of our survival instinct that feels it is necessary to identify and handle threats to our wellbeing.

Let's further consider the fearful, anxious student mentioned above. If the student develops a sense of mindfulness and evaluates their situation without judgment, they may use their observations to identify that trigger for themselves. Once they realize that the exam triggered the fearful anxious reaction and that they are scared because failure may mean not going to college, they can focus on a plan to convert that energy into positive acceptance, scheduled worry time, distractions or even planning for success.

Other triggers for these behaviors may include visible competition with others. When our failure is public and not just private, the consequences can seem so much bigger, and this naturally drives the anxiety level higher. Anything that causes uncertainty for the future can trigger nervousness and anxiety. Things that challenge our self-confidence and make us confront perceived challenges or shortcomings can also trigger a negative emotional state.

Let's use an example from the workplace. An upcoming project deadline may be causing you an undue amount of stress and anxiety. You have started to act nervous and jittery and are having trouble concentrating on your work. Furthermore, you are not able to function effectively at home due to your preoccupation with the project. When you do a careful self-examination, you may discover that the anxiety you are feeling has been triggered by a fear of failure, because your project teammate and you are both being evaluated for a promotion. You may not have told your domestic partner, and you don't want to get their hopes up. You don't want them to see you as a failure and are worried they will be disappointed in you.

Whenever you have an activity or task where the consequences of the outcome are significant to you, it is natural to be nervous. When that nervousness turns into debilitating anxiety, it is critically important to identify the source of your anxiety and take positive steps to manage it. This benefits both you and your loved ones, who may be troubled by your emotional or physical state and want to help you.

Studying and identifying your triggers and understanding the root causes of your anxiety are the only way you can move beyond them and transform the negative physical responses into positive energy.

Transforming Anxiety And Nervousness Into Excitement

Understanding the root causes of your anxiety, recognizing your triggers and using coping techniques previously discussed, you are well-positioned to consider the challenge of transforming your negative, nervous, anxious energy into the positive energy of excitement. This is not to be undertaken with the belief that it is easy, and it doesn't just happen because you want it to. You have to maintain constant awareness of your state of mind and body and be able to redirect that energy when you feel it coming over you. It may sound exhausting but once you have trained your body to redirect itself, it will require little effort. As with many things, "practice makes perfect". You may consider the occurrence of such anxious behaviors as a downfall. However, with the right tools and attitude, it is also possible for you to be able to turn the anxieties and nervousness into something positive and useful.

There are various ways to approach transforming negative nervousness into excitement. One method was developed by Cung Khuu, a personal development writer (Khuu, 2018). He discusses the fact that we often try to go from anxiety to calm. This is very hard to do since the emotional and physical responses to anxiety and calm are so different. On the other hand, since anxiety and excitement are so similar in how the body reacts, it is easier to convince the mind that the feelings are tied to something positive.

He suggested that you can reduce anxieties and nervousness through self-development, determination and the following of four simple steps. It starts with the simple statement of "get excited". Some people are able to make that switch easily. They feel the symptoms of nervousness coming on, such as sudden flashes of hot or cold, nausea or jittery movements. Then they say to themselves, "I'm not nervous, I'm excited!" and they then think about all the potential positive outcomes of the situation instead of the negative ones.

Cung Khuu suggests that when you are in a situation that makes you nervous or anxious, and you are not able to convert your negative energy into positive excitement, you should follow four simple steps. Let's identify the steps, explain them, and then consider the ways that we can use them to move from nervousness and anxiety to excitement.

Embrace The Emotions

Take the time to examine your physical and emotional response. Recognize how you feel. Are you hyperventilating, are you sweating, are you jittery and can't stop moving, or are you unable to move because you feel so ill? Give the emotions a moment of thanks for making you so aware of the potential dangers to you, and then recognize how these symptoms are similar to excitement. In talking about embracing your emotions, Cung Khuu, encourages you not to fight the emotions you are experiencing. This does not mean you should encourage the escalation of the emotional or physical condition. This is to help you identify it and deal with it within a shorter period of time. You may tell yourself, "wow, this is how I'm feeling and that is legitimate, but I will only let my mind and body indulge in this behavior for a designated period of time". After all, the expression "time heals everything" is indicative of the diminishing impact of anxiety on our body the further we move away in time from the triggering event. Giving it recognition makes it less mysterious, and that gives it less power over you.

In addition to embracing the emotions, it is also important that you conduct positive self-talk and try to convert your feelings into positive manifestations of excitement. Making deliberately positive statements about yourself or your situation has immediate benefits to your emotional and physical state. Tell yourself nice things and believe them! Invest your energy in thoughts of personal development and the embracing of positive ideas.

Most people can understand that someone who is in mourning is naturally consumed with grief and may cry for long periods of time. That is an example of accepting the emotions and allowing yourself to go through them. Most people also understand that at some point you have to move beyond that emotion to another state of mind. Although this is different from embracing the anxious responses of the body to stress, it is a good example of how people have been encouraged to embrace emotion, give it value, space and time in an effort to move beyond the emotion into a different one. Recognizing the intensity of your emotions without judgment is less burdensome on the psyche than criticizing yourself for the perceived weakness of succumbing to negative emotions. Facing your emotional state head-on is usually a better way to deal with it, and by doing so, you have a higher potential of being able to redirect that energy.

Stop Beating Yourself Up

You are really hard on yourself. Sometimes the things we are nervous about are out of our control and we must simply wait for an outcome. The outcome will be the same whether you worry about it or not. Stop focusing on all the ways you believe you have caused your own demise or all the ways things could go wrong. Stop it! Remember to tell yourself that despite any perceived obstacles, there are many advantages to putting your worries aside. You have made efforts towards your goal, and you deserve to congratulate yourself on that.

Cung Khuu also encourages us not to be so deeply consumed by the negative thoughts that we have. Nervousness and other signs of anxiety are often an outward expression of overthinking. When these symptoms are acute and debilitating, they may be at a point where they are dangerous to your health. You may develop additional negative symptoms such as migraines or even have a heart attack or experience dangerous spikes in your blood pressure that could lead to a stroke. These are serious medical conditions that may be avoided if you properly manage your anxiety.

Don't beat yourself up for not achieving everything you want to right now. Stop beating yourself up over the fact that you are not dealing with your stress and anxiety very well. Give yourself a break! Sometimes things happen that we are unable to control, but we are able to control our reaction to them if we give ourselves the chance to move beyond our emotional state.

For example, imagine a college student who has an academic scholarship and is fully sponsored by an organization. The money the student receives is just enough to pay the bills, and there is none left over to save for an emergency. At some point, the scholarship money is delayed due to an administrative error at the institution's accounting department. For this reason, the student is unable to pay their rent because they have not received the money in time. When they tell the landlord what happened, they are threatened with eviction if they don't pay on time. In order to meet their financial obligations, they decide to borrow money from their parents because they are worried about eviction for non-payment. This situation would be very upsetting to many people. Some people would escalate their negative feelings to include berating themselves. They might berate themselves for failure to manage their money, the nervousness of asking for a financial loan, and the anxiety of potentially losing their housing. Once you recognize that you have these feelings ask yourself if you are being unduly hard on yourself. Stop beating yourself up! For example, you can confidently tell yourself that everything is okay because you did not fail to manage your money. The scholarship money failed to arrive on time. That was not because of anything you did. Furthermore, your parents had the money to lend and understood that it was just a temporary cash-flow problem caused by no fault of your own. To continue in this vein, there is no reason to be anxious about getting evicted because you were able to secure the loan to pay your rent. You should feel good about how you recognized the problem in time, rallied your resources, and solved the issue before it had any truly negative consequences for you.

Try To Convince Yourself You Are Excited

Make a conscious effort to reframe your emotions. Your body currently believes that these emotions are a reaction to negative stimuli; dangers that we must be protected from. What if your body believed that these physical responses were a sign of excitement due to the potential of something good happening? Tell yourself why this is exciting. Could the outcome have positive benefits for you? What are all the good things that could come out of it? Instead of the emotions signaling impending doom, tell your body those emotions signal the approach of a new exciting opportunity.

Sometimes our mind and body develop an attachment to the relationship between stimuli and reaction and it is familiar, though may not be comfortable. The body immediately responds in the same way to the same triggers. When we feel anxious and nervous, we are often thinking about all the negative potential of a situation and all the ways in which we could fail or let ourselves down. For this reason, the body and mind are associating this kind of situation and the emotions you feel with a negative outcome.

Because of this tendency of the body and mind to go to the most familiar place, it can be hard to redirect those feelings and have breakthroughs in challenging situations. Instead of going to the same negative place in our mind, when you are feeling anxious and nervous, think consciously of all the ways the situation could be successful and work out for you. Then your body will start to associate those same feelings with the positivity of success.

You need to convince yourself that at that moment of distress, the feelings are the signal of the beginning of an exciting thing yet to come. It can be hard not to focus on the negative because it is so powerful and occupies so much of our consciousness. It may take some time, but you can train yourself to recognize the negative feelings of anxiety and nervousness and convert them into a state of excitement. You will stop dreading those feelings and start using them as a way to bring more excitement into your life.

Visualize Success

People often talk about visualization, and there is a reason why it is so popular as a tool for accomplishing many great and challenging things. Visualization is an effective tool for moving our brain from negative to positive places. When we imagine all the ways in which we could succeed at our endeavor, and what that would look like, our emotional state switches from negative nervousness and anxiety to a state of positive excitement and anticipation.

To get past negative emotions, we must take the time to consciously do something different with our minds and imagination. Instead of imaging all the things that could go wrong, imaging all the things that could go right. This will help convert your emotional energy from negative to positive because of the power of association discussed above.

You may have to work very hard to transform your perception of yourself and concentrate on the possible success that might come from the situation you are in. Focus on visualizing yourself being on the other side of the anxiety and feeling better. Imagine how far forward you can move if you focus on moving towards the successful resolution of your situation. This is something that you can do to effectively get yourself to the point where you recognize the triggers of your anxiety and can redirect your thoughts before they have a negative impact on you.

Chapter Summary

In this chapter, we learned that it is possible to convert anxiety and nervousness into a state of excitement.

In order to do that, we must first review and understand what the triggers are for our anxiety, and how they manifest in physical responses by our body. Anxiety and nervousness may be expressed by the body in the form of shaking, jittery movements or speech, short breaths, hot flashes and nausea. You may also experience an increased heart rate, restlessness, and insomnia. Coincidentally, those are also some of the symptoms of excitement.

Cung Khuu, a personal development writer, espouses the transformation of nervousness and anxiety into excitement. He teaches people a very useful set of tasks that can lead you to that positive place. These four steps require you to:

- embrace your emotions.
- stop beating yourself up.
- tell yourself to get excited.
- visualize success.

Learning to convert your negative emotions and physical reactions to stress into something more positive like excitement has many long-term health benefits, both physically and emotionally. Untethered stress and anxiety can lead to many of the modern killer diseases like heart attack and stroke.

Do not despair if at first you find it difficult to convert your anxiety and nervousness into excitement. It may take some time to train your body to recognize and redirect negative emotions and physical responses into a more positive place, but you will get there.

In the next chapter, you will learn about the importance of making a list of joyful activities and then engaging in them...

CHAPTER SEVEN:

Making Your List of Joyful Activities

In this chapter, you are going to learn about how making the conscious decision to seek out joy in our lives can have many benefits. When we accept joy into our lives, it takes up space in our emotional and physical landscape. Depending on how much space and time we allocate to joy, there is less room for anxiety, nervousness, and the debilitating effects that overthinking can have on our wellbeing. When we make time and room in our lives to find and experience joy, we are making ourselves available for the positive feelings it brings with it.

As you clearly know, we are all very different people, who go through different things in life. It is important to remember that although the specifics of what we are going through may vary, there are likely general similarities with the experiences of others. We all have some degree of worry over finances, success, health, etc. We all have different ways of dealing with the issues we face. Some people are able to accept these challenges with calm and grace. Others may ruminate excessively, have panic attacks or experience surges in emotional stability. Some people may take longer to find a way out of their difficult situations. Others may have instant and definite solutions. Either way, we must all commit to moving toward the resolution of our concerns in a way that is healthy for our body and mind.

As a result of the amount of time and energy we spend on the emotions and symptoms of anxiety and obsessive overthinking, we may have little time to think about anything else. There comes a point when it may be necessary to make the decision to make room in your consciousness for the experience of joy.

Making Room For Joy

When you are able to experience a joyful or enjoyable event, it causes surges of endorphins which make you feel good. Furthermore, your body may relax, your mind might clear, you might laugh or smile and your nervousness will subside. These overall effects result in a more positive outlook on life. During the time that you were "having fun", you were not thinking about your anxiety. Isn't that a relief?

We all have different things that bring us true joy. You may have very specific things that trigger feelings of happiness and joy. We have focussed on negative triggers for much of this book, but let's take a moment to talk about positive triggers. There are some things that we may have done in the past that we know bring us joy, enjoyment or excitement. It is time to call upon those memories, and if possible, recreate them. For example, you may have a favorite song that you associate with a particularly fun evening you had. Whenever you hear that song, you are instantly transported to that memory, and your body experiences those feelings of joy again. These are positive triggers. You may love to swim, and every time you drive past a recreation center with a pool, your body remembers how good it feels to dive in that first time when you get there.

Develop An Inventory

We previously discussed making a list of the things that cause you anxiety. For similar reasons, it is useful to make a list of the things that cause you joy, give you enjoyment or that get you excited when you think about them or engage in doing them.

When you have a list to refer to, it can make it easier to make positive decisions when you are in a challenging situation. Consider it your "finding joy cheat sheet".

Don't be shy. Take the time to self-evaluate. It may not be easy because you have had so little joy in your life recently that you can't remember clearly what things you used to enjoy. Maybe you feel like even if you could make a list, it wouldn't matter because you don't have either the time, money or energy to do those things. That's okay. Make the list anyway. You can sort it into categories later and use it to make plans. The list has all sorts of uses. For example, you can use it as a trigger to just remember good things, which will have an immediate positive impact on your outlook. If the list is short at first, just add to it as you think of things. You can even put things on the list that you think you might enjoy and try them to see if you liked it. Don't feel as if the things on the list need to cost money to do. There are a lot of enjoyable things that you can do that are free.

Maybe what gives you joy or enjoyment is not the same as it is for other people. In fact, that is what makes these lists so interesting. You might be surprised at the things you put on there. Maybe it is a special food or a special song or hiking with your special someone. Maybe it is planting seeds in your garden. Maybe it is watching birds. It doesn't matter what is on the list, as long as you are honest with yourself about what gives you enjoyment. This is because this list is your own personal toolbox. The items on this list will become the go-to things that you can draw upon when you need to reorient your mental and physical state.

After you have made your list, make a plan to incorporate those activities into your life. Whatever you do, make time to actively engage in activities that make you feel good. In addition to giving you the opportunity to experience positive emotions, there is less room for the influence of anxiety on your life. Also, because you are in a more positive mental and physical state, you are more resilient to the triggers that you might encounter.

There are some activities that are commonly enjoyed either alone or with others, and these may be a starting place for your list if you are having trouble getting started.

Activities That Might Be Enjoyable

Once you have conducted the appropriate self-reflection, you will have a list to work with. This list should only be of things that bring you joy, enjoyment or excitement. These are things that have the ability to knock you out of your negative state and put a smile on your face or make you happy in some way. For the items that you know to give you joy, make a point to schedule them into your life. Don't leave it to chance that you will spontaneously make time to engage in your preferred activities. You have to actually do the things on your list to get the full benefit. It is okay to just think about them and use it to remember when you were feeling joy, but it is even more powerful if you go through the experience again and recreate those feelings so they are fresh in your mind and you can have the benefit of the actual physical reaction that can be so transformative.

Let's review some of the things that are commonly done to bring people joy, enjoyment, peace, contentment and other positive emotions. Some of these activities might not be of interest to you at first but do consider trying new things. You might be surprised what your body reacts to. Many of these activities are regularly used by people seeking to bring more joy into their lives.

Watching A Funny Movie Or Show

It is often said that laughter is the best medicine. That is really true! While some people say that watching any show is a distraction, shows that are funny have a way of transforming our mood. They have a way of making us forget our troubles, and they let us just sink into another reality. Before you know it, you are laughing at a joke and you get a rush of endorphins. Success! You have switched your mind from a state of anxiety to a state of joy. You may notice that your physical tension drains away and you are less jittery and irritable. You might not have thought about your problems for a whole half hour! If you resolve to do this once a day at least, you will be able to look forward to this time when you will be treating yourself to the emotional and physical benefits of laughter. If you need a longer dose of light-hearted laughter, try a comedy stand-up special or a comedy movie. Even if you find them "stupid" or "infantile", don't underestimate the value of those couple of laughs you might indulge in. Even if you don't get a lot of laughs, you will have spent time not thinking about your problems. If your problems keep seeping to the forefront despite watching these shows, don't despair, try a different show or comedian.

Sometimes we can get a great benefit from watching any kind of movie or show that takes our mind off our problems. It is important not to choose shows that will upset you, trigger negative memories, or remind you too much of your own situation. The idea is to add positive input to your life. Maybe you find it easier to lose yourself in a good action film, or a nice romance. As long as you are feeling good when you watch it, you are on the right track. This is why it is important to try different things, and variations of different things until you are fully successful in identifying the perfect go-to activity when you need to be lifted up.

Spend Time Doing Or Appreciating Artistic Activities

Over history, some of the world's best artistic works, and especially paintings, were done by artists in a profound emotional state. They may have been in love, happy and well-fed, or they could have been persecuted, angry and poor. Some were even bored and just making something on a commission that didn't inspire them at all. The artist may have had an easy upbringing in a country that is at peace, or the artist could have grown up the offspring of a revolutionary, fighting for human rights in their country. All of these factors influence the emotion that is expressed in the art we look at. As with the extreme emotions that may lead to the creation of a genius work of art, the viewing of incredible art can evoke strong and profound emotions and physical reactions in us. We may look at a painting and get a sense of longing or contentment from it. For someone else, it might be boring. Another might give us joy because it shows a subject that is dear to our heart, like a child with a puppy or a smiling woman collecting shells on a sunny beach.

You don't have to have a lot of money to be an appreciator of art. Some of the best art is on display in free galleries and museums. Also, libraries and used bookstores have a huge selection of books on art that you can look at and experience at your leisure. Walk into an open art gallery or artisan gift shop wherever you live. Take out books from the library that display art from various eras and artists.

When you are exposed to artwork, you will find that you have an emotional reaction to some of them. When you find images that make you feel happy or joyful, take note of them, and return to them often in order to recreate that good feeling you have when looking at it. If you are able to get a copy of the art piece or image, it may be advantageous to display it in a section of your home where you can see it often. This way, you will have many opportunities to recreate the feeling of joy that you got when looking at it the first time.

A lot of emotion goes into creating art and making your own art can be an excellent way to generate a regular influx of joy into our lives.

Creating art is an impactful outlet for your negative energy, and it can be a way to bring more positivity into your world. If you are angry, you may be able to express this anger, and purge it from your system by making an intense art piece that demonstrates your emotional state. Artists are often able to communicate the emotions they are going through in their paintings, sculptures and other artistic works.

Paintings, drawings, sculptures, photos, tapestries, and other art forms can express anger, confusion, anxiety, despair, horror and a wide range of negative emotions. They can also express love, admiration, calm, adoration, joy, amusement, and other positive emotions. Just as artists throughout the centuries have used art as an outlet for their emotional and physical energy, you can benefit from using the creation of art as an outlet for you to release negativity and invite in joy.

You do not need to even be a good artist to use this tool, nor do you ever need to show anyone what you have created. You don't even have to keep what you have created. You just have to commit to putting your feelings into the art instead of internalizing them. It is the act of internalizing our negative emotions, often through overthinking, rumination and self-doubt that causes our body and mind to express signs of distress.

Think about the thing that is upsetting you and create something that expresses this for you. It can even be abstract and look like nothing at all. As long as you use this as a chance to channel the distress you are feeling into the art. This is you giving it time and a voice. When you are finished, you can walk away and think about other things, or nothing at all. This opportunity to expel the emotions from your body can be very freeing, as it gives you an opportunity to let go of those emotions and "leave them on the canvas".

Art can be a powerful outlet for negative emotions, but many people prefer to focus on positive thoughts when they create art. They do this in order to invite joy and contentment into their lives. They may enjoy the act of creating something, no matter what it is. They may try to recreate something they find beautiful or calming, and in recreating the calming image, they are able to bring calm into their own body and mind. The act of creating something can have positive benefits to your perspective and your self-esteem. There is joy and pride in saying, "I made that". Every time you look at the item you created, you have an opportunity to recreate positive emotions associated with joy and personal pride. Maybe you tried and you don't think you are good enough to keep going. Don't sell yourself short. It is the act of creation that is important, not the quality of the result. You don't even have to keep it if you don't want, but you will always have the pride of spending that time completely engrossed in trying to create something beautiful and joyful.

When you go looking, you will find some amazing art, including paintings, drawings, photographs, tapestries, sculptures and many crazy fun crafts. Open your mind to artforms you may not have seen or tried before. You may be surprised what brings you joy. Exploring the art of others can inspire you to try creating art of your own. You might see or try something new and find that you like it very much and that it brings joy or other positive emotions into your life. Regardless of what art form you choose to make, use it as a tool to purge negative emotions and express or create positive emotions.

Listen To And Make Music

We've all said, "oh, I love that song!" at some point when a song we like comes on. We are filled instantly with feelings of joy, a smile comes over our face, and we might start tapping our toes or even start dancing a little. That is what spontaneous joy feels like, and we should endeavor to repeat those feelings whenever we can. It is hard to focus on our anxiety when we are singing along to an upbeat song.

Listening to music is a great way to give yourself something to do besides worry. In order to be truly effective though, you have to listen actively, and not let your mind wander. It is best when you can sing along, as this fully engages your body in the activity. Not only can you hear the music, but the act of singing creates endorphin surges that have beneficial effects on our breathing and we are more likely to move around. If you are somewhere you can't sing along, listen intently to the words and the music. Try to think only of the lyrics and the beats, and don't let your mind wander.

Further to the act of listening to music is the act of making music. It can be very joyful to play an instrument, even if you are not very good at it. If you have the opportunity, practice making music. It is a great distraction since it fills your mind and body with the need to focus on a specific activity. You may also be singing, which fully engages the mind and body to the exclusion of negative thoughts. Maybe you used to play an instrument in school but haven't played in years. Try to find that instrument at a thrift shop and start playing again. You would be surprised how fast it comes back to you. Maybe you have always wanted to learn a specific instrument. Get one and start learning. The internet and the library have lots of resources if you don't want to spend money on lessons. Maybe you were given or you inherited an instrument from a friend or family. This is the perfect opportunity to try something new.

If you have no access to instruments, drumming is a great option, because you can use anything as a drum, and use either your hands, cutlery or chopsticks to tap on the surface. Just tapping along on the table to the beat of a song that you like can be tremendously enjoyable and is highly recommended.

There is one very important thing to remember about using music to change your mood. You have to make sure to listen to and play upbeat, cheerful, or hopeful songs. When you are anxious about finances or the potential of losing your job, a sad song about someone who just went broke may sink you deeper into despair.

At the heart of this plan to use music to find joy is that you must find music that resonates joyfully within you, and repeatedly expose yourself to it, so that you have more joy in your life.

Do Some Charity Work

Sometimes the best way to distract ourselves from our problems, or transform our emotional state is to help others. This is especially true if you are consumed by nervous energy and need an outlet for it. Similarly, when you are focussed on helping others, your mind and body is too busy to worry about your own problems. Sometimes seeing the problems of others gives you perspective about your own situation, and you feel better about where you are in life. Sometimes you can meet other really great, genuine and caring people who are also doing charity work. These are the positive types of people that you want to be around.

When we help others, we can derive a great sense of pride from a job well done, or from seeing the joy on someone else's face when they get something good that they weren't expecting. Stress and anxiety can often be replaced by joy and happiness when we involve ourselves in charity activities. It does not matter if you only have a little time to give, find a charity in your community that you feel passionate about, and offer them your time. When most people think about charity work, they automatically think of food banks and soup kitchens, but that is only a tiny fraction of the organizations that could use your help. If you are good with kids and youths, you may want to be involved in a youth mentoring program or community center. If you are good with animals and they give you joy, you may want to volunteer at a local animal shelter to walk dogs or play with cats. Help raise money for or participate in environmental clean-ups. Type out letters for the elderly or help them with their shopping. This may involve giving your time and energy to others, but since you were just wasting it on being anxious, use it to help others.

Giving hope to other people and putting smiles on the faces of others is very rewarding and creates a variety of positive emotions for us, and this translates into less anxiety. There is a lot of satisfaction to be had when you make a positive impact in the life of another person.

Attend More Social Gatherings

Many people just love their own company and prefer to be alone. Sometimes people don't love their own company but are nervous about interacting with others. Sometimes we just get so busy that we don't make time for people outside of our immediate circle of family and co-workers. Either way, being alone too much or not making time for socializing can have a very detrimental effect on our emotional health. It is easy to stay wrapped up in your anxiety when you are alone and have no other opinions or perspectives to interrupt your negative thought patterns. If you suffer from anxiety, there can be many benefits to getting out of your solitary state where you are likely ruminating upon all the things that make you anxious.

If, for whatever reason, you don't have friends to socialize with, there are still many opportunities in the community for social interaction. Socializing can be as simple as starting a conversation with the counter attendant at your grocery store. It can be as simple as having coffee with a colleague at lunch. It can be as extravagant as accepting an invitation to a dinner party or a mixer for work or attending a wedding. You might also be able to join a local club or class at a community center. These are all ways to engage socially with others and give ourselves the opportunity to experience enjoyment.

When we have positive interactions with others it takes our mind off the source of our anxiety. We may find that listening to others speak exposes us to things that are interesting or amusing. Also, when we see that others are able to enjoy our company and that we are interacting well with others, it gives us an increased sense of self-worth and opens us up to feeling more joyful about ourselves and our situation.

When we "step out and socialize", attend public meetings or events, we are assailed by a whole new set of stimuli, and some of them may result in feelings of enjoyment. We may meet someone interesting and learn something new. We may hear someone tell a really funny story and it makes us laugh. We may have an opportunity to watch some really skilled musicians play and maybe even dance. This will cause the influx of positive emotions and get our body into a different physical and emotional state.

Going to a social event, or even the thought of going to social events, may be something that you find stressful and anxiety causing in itself, so you will have to work through that or make decisions that you are comfortable with. You may be terrified to go out and interact with others due to your anxiety, but ironically, that may be the best way out of your poor emotional state. Embrace opportunities for social gatherings, and if you find them difficult, work on becoming progressively more tolerant of the extra stimuli and getting used to trying to interact with others. Tell yourself that you don't have to stay, you just have to go and try. If you have a positive interaction, you might just find yourself sticking around.

Family And Friends Time

Family can be an important part of our support structure. We may depend on family for various things, and some people have more family support than others. When we have a supportive family, we are able to count on them to be a part of our lives. This interaction with people who love us can be a source of great joy and enjoyment. You may really enjoy listening to your grandmother tell stories about the old days, and it may give you a different perspective about how hard your life is. Your uncle might have great advice for you about how he handled a stressful situation once. You might see a cousin who expresses a mutual interest in a music group or artist. Someone might remind of a really funny thing that happened, or they might give you a hug or tell you that they are proud of you. Sometimes they may do nothing other than be company that you can count on. These are all family situations that can bring us joy if we embrace them.

Some families and family homes may not be supportive and welcoming and healthy for you. When this is the case, seek out other family type groups. There are many different types of families, and many "family members" may not be biologically related. Some people consider their friends as their family and trust them more than anyone. The important thing is that you spend time with the people who you trust, who support you, and who you enjoy spending time with. These should be people that bring out the happiness in you, not the ones who bring you down with constant negativity.

If you have friends, this can be the best social outlet and an effective way to "cheer you up". Socializing with someone you know and trust is the best way to create opportunities for meaningful positive interaction. Being with someone who is non-judgemental of us, and who knows how to "cheer us up" can be a great resource. Be sure to use these opportunities to do fun things together and do not use it as an opportunity to focus on your anxieties out loud. The point of social engagement is to get us out of our negative headspace and fill that space with happy and joyful things. This can include all sorts of things like playing a game with your friend, watching a funny show together, taking a walk, going to a gallery or to a music venue, or eating some amazing food that you cooked together.

Interacting With Nature

One of the most profound ways to change your negative mindset and counteract the symptoms of anxiety and nervousness is to spend time outside in nature. Taking the time to go outside and breathe fresh air gives us an opportunity to clear our head and move our bodies, and to see beautiful things. When we go to the park or interact with the natural world, we may enjoy the feeling of the wind in our hair, find contentment in a good stretch, find laughter in watching a dog chase after a toy, or find wonder in the beauty of a flower. Forests of any kind are rejuvenating and can bring us to a place of wonder as we contemplate the interconnectedness of the species of flora and fauna that exist there together.

The Japanese have a practice called Shinrin-yoku which literally means "forest bath" You and I know it as a "walk in the woods". Japanese researchers measured changes in the bodies of people who walked for about 20 minutes in a beautiful forest, with the woodsy smells and the sounds of a running stream. The "forest bathers" had lower stress hormone levels after their walk than they did after a comparable walk in an urban area, and that these effects lasted up to a month. (Li, 2018; Livni, 2016)

There is no doubt of the calming effects of walking in a park, forest or garden. Camping and hiking are wonderful opportunities to focus our minds on something bigger than ourselves. When we interact with nature, we can see ourselves as a smaller part of an interconnected world. The positive aromatherapy benefits of being in an environment that smells fresh and of trees and flowers are tremendous. While we are in the natural environment, we are likely walking around, and this physical movement causes surges of positive endorphins and can give us an outlet for our nervous energy.

Challenges That May Be Faced When Seeking Joy

There are many things that we can do in an effort to bring more joy into our lives. We have explored some very effective and common activities that are known to be effective in lifting people's spirits and transforming anxiety into joy.

It is important to acknowledge the fact that not all of these activities will be enjoyable to all people. Explore different activities and keep building your list of things to do. Try what you think will bring you the most, or even some, joy.

You need to be careful and sensitive with yourself when you take on activities in an attempt to deliberately challenge your body and mind to find enjoyment. For example, if we have a terrible fear of heights, accepting an invitation for lunch on a rooftop patio might be more than you can handle, and you should not add to your stress by attempting to confront that fear when you are simply trying to find some joy in lunch out with a friend. In this scenario a true friend will understand when you say, "if it's okay with you, I would be more comfortable in a restaurant that is on ground level".

When you reach that level where you are able to confidently identify the things that hinder you from achieving joy, you may have to carefully come up with ways to eliminate them from your life. Forming habits at your workplace or home that progressively eliminate your exposure to negative stimuli and increase your exposure to positive stimuli will result in a greater degree of joy and happiness.

Chapter Summary

We all deserve to be happy and to experience joy. In order to maximize your potential for joy, you need to always be on the lookout for both the things that you know trigger anxiety, and also for the things that trigger joy. Increasing our exposure to the things that trigger joy for us has a transformative effect on our emotional state and on the emotional and physical expression of anxiety.

Often, we are consumed with negative thoughts and our anxiety may be at a peak. When this happens, you must make a conscious effort to expose yourself to the things that give you joy. Once you make a decision to make room in your life for joy, you may need to develop a plan of how to do that. We may have forgotten what gives us joy because we have been anxious for so long. We may have few resources at our disposal for doing things that cost money. That's why making a list is so important. The list may be small at first and it may take a while to get enough things on it that you feel you have a lot of options. Put things on the list that you think might be enjoyable. Put anything on the list that you can think of, and then just start trying things that are appropriate at the time. The truth is you really only need to start with one thing. Be on the lookout for the things that increase your anxiety and sap your happiness and joy, and then do away with as many of them as you can.

Some of the joyful activities that we've discussed include watching funny shows, spending time on artistic endeavors, listening to music, attending social gatherings, and others. Embrace these opportunities to experience joy and repeat them as much as you can. This will keep the anxiety at bay, because your emotions and your body are engaged in something else that is keeping you focused on positive things.

In the next chapter, you will learn more about the many natural remedies for anxiety...

CHAPTER EIGHT:

Natural Remedies to Beat Anxiety

Sometimes the best remedies for the anxious mind and body is a proper regime of healthy choices in various areas of our lives. These choices are largely in the area of self-care, and they may include a commitment to a healthy lifestyle that includes exercise and the proper diet.

Self-Care

Generally speaking, when you are in a state of heightened anxiety, your self-care regimes may be pushed aside in favor of rumination and panic, self-doubt and the attempt to accomplish everything that we set out to do. When we are too busy or too preoccupied with our anxiety, we may stop taking care of ourselves properly. We may let our bodies get run down, stop exercising, cut back on sleep or sleep poorly, and we may not eat properly. This compounds the negative effects of anxiety because our body is less resilient to the impacts of stress.

For example, if you have a deadline, or many things on the go at once, you may be pressed for time and be very anxious about achieving your goal. Since so much depends on the result of your efforts, you may have stayed up late many nights in a row in order to work or study, and maybe you've been eating fast snacks instead of cooking yourself nutritious meals. You also have probably been sitting in the same position without stretching for long periods of time. You may be berating yourself constantly and doubting your ability to accomplish your goal.

These are all examples of ways that we neglect to provide ourselves with self-care. The truth is, if you were sleeping more regularly, eating better and stretching at regular intervals, your symptoms of anxiety would probably be lessened.

There are many ways to increase our level of self-care, and we will explore some of them below.

Exercise

It is important for all of us to prioritize being healthy as a partial antidote to anxiety. We all yearn to live a healthy life, and this is especially true when old age begins to set in. With that in mind, create a plan that will ensure you remain healthy. One of the keys to good health is exercise. You may have heard this many times before, but you need to believe it and embrace it. There are many ways to exercise and you need to find the one that is best for you. Whatever you do, try to make it fun by choosing the right activities and approaching them with a good attitude, confident in the knowledge that this healthy choice will have many positive impacts upon the management of your anxiety symptoms.

You may be able to join a gym, or you may want to exercise alone at home or use the park or a community facility. The important thing is that you get your body moving and stretching and that you get your heart rate up, and that you breathe regularly and deeply. There are so many ways to do that.

If you have access to or can acquire home gym or exercise equipment of any kind, that is the best and easiest way to integrate exercise into your life. When it is at home and easily accessible, it is easy to schedule it into your daily life. Try exercising right before you get into the shower, or when you get home from work or school. This is a great way to get out your tension and channel any negative energy into a good workout. When you exercise, your body releases endorphins and that makes us feel good. Even doing a few minutes a day, or ten minutes every couple of days is better than nothing and will get you in the habit of exercising. At first, it may be hard to go longer than a few minutes, but if you keep at it regularly, you will find it easier as you become more fit. It is often helpful to listen to music or an audiobook when exercising. This is to keep you distracted from thinking about your problems while you exercise. Practicing mindfulness can also be helpful. Focus on your muscles, on your breathing and on your posture as you exercise, whatever it is. How do you feel? Fully experience the joy of your body working in a healthy, natural way.

There are many ways to exercise at home without "formal gym equipment". If you need ideas and instruction about exercises and stretches that might work for you, go to the library or the internet to research your many options.

If you want to, and are able to make it work, join a gym or register for exercise classes at a gym or community center and attend them faithfully. This may have the added benefit of social interactions that could lead to positive and interesting friendships, or at least some positive light socializing.

If you prefer to exercise outdoors, walking, hiking or running can be a great way to exercise. Maybe you have a back yard you can use to do an exercise routine or a basketball hoop you can use to shoot hoops. Taking a football/soccer ball to kick around at a park or a tennis ball to bounce around at public court can be a great way to release pent up nervous energy and anxiety.

Doing regular exercise has the added benefit of controlling your weight and helping to regulate your blood sugar, thus promoting better health. Remember, a healthy body is more resilient to stress.

There is an endless list of activities that you may consider when exploring self-care through exercise. Try to do something you enjoy, but whatever you do, do something. If you love to swim, find a way to swim regularly. If you enjoy dancing, do it regularly. If you enjoy hiking through an urban forest, do that regularly. Channel your anxiety and nervousness into intensifying your workout and be mindful of the way your body feels as you get healthier.

Exercise is a powerful antidote to anxiety and depression and has both immediate and long- term benefits.

The 21-minute Cure

Dr. Drew Ramsey, assistant clinical professor of psychiatry at the New York-Presbyterian Hospital at Columbia University and co-author of "*The Happiness Diet*" says that in order for exercise to have a beneficial effect on anxiety, you should engage in it for about twenty-one minutes. (Barnett, 2019). He attests to the fact that you will feel calmer after the workout. He asks his patients to spend 20 to 30 minutes doing any activity that gets their heart rate up. It can be anything they like, whether it's a treadmill, elliptical or rowing, or even brisk walks.

Resolve To Eat A Healthy Diet

Another secret to successful self-care and the use of self-care to reduce anxiety is adhering to a healthy diet. The ability of our body to regulate hormones and to function effectively and make us feel healthy is largely influenced by the things that we eat and drink.

We can all understand the connection between bad food decisions and stomach distress, but few people fail to associate the impact of poor-quality food on other aspects of our physical and psychological health. Furthermore, few people give credit to nutritious food as being one of the building blocks of general good health, both physically and psychologically.

When our body receives a good balance of proteins, vegetables, fruits, and grains, it is able to function at its prime. This in return makes it more able to cope with stress, which minimizes the symptoms of anxiety.

Commit to eating more fruits and vegetables. Fresh is always best since fresh fruits and vegetables have the highest amount of nutrients and fiber.

Foods that are highly processed and/or are high in sugar, salt and additives should be avoided. It is well known that high sugar intake is harmful to our bodies and can lead to conditions such as obesity and diabetes. It is also known that high salt intake can contribute to conditions such as high blood pressure.

Furthermore, the intake of caffeine-based and sugary drinks should be minimized, especially from late afternoon to bedtime.

Sometimes it can be hard to make good food decisions when we are away from the controlled environment of our own home. We may be assailed with options that seem more attractive than others, or we may not have access to healthy choices because of limited options. Sometimes we are too busy to cook and find ourselves bringing home takeout, ordering in, or just grabbing something on the run to eat in the car. These are the times when we can do the most damage to our health, as these foods tend to be high in saturated fats, sugar, salt, additives, preservatives and other artificial or highly processed ingredients.

These occasions where we have to get quick or convenient food can be minimized by good planning. For example, if you know you are going to be busy running around, pack a nutritious snack or lunch. Sometimes, however, eating out or eating on the run can't be avoided. When this happens, get in the habit of making the healthiest choice you can. At first, it may be hard to get over the automatic instinct to, for example, get fries. This is the moment when you must choose the salad and not smother it completely in dressing. Choose grilled instead of fried. Choose soda, water or juice instead of cola or coffee. If you are in a restaurant, choose your meal carefully, and make the healthiest choice you can. A lean grilled or poached protein, with salad or cooked vegetables, are available almost everywhere.

Quick, Eat Something

Dr. Ramsey and many others confirm that people's levels of anxiety and irritability increase when they are hungry. When you get overwhelmed with anxiety, it may be a sign that your blood sugar is low. Have a quick, healthy snack, like a handful of nuts and raisins, along with a glass of water or a nice hot beverage.

Don't Skip Breakfast

You are often encouraged to eat a healthy breakfast. Many people insist they aren't hungry in the morning or skip breakfast because they are so busy in the morning. A healthy daily breakfast is one of the most important tools you can give your body to work with. Skipping breakfast is a guaranteed way to find yourself suddenly hungry at an inopportune time. For example, getting to work hungry is an assured recipe for a stressful day in the office, or an inability to deal with stressors. You may feel weak or emotionally fragile, have trouble concentrating, be irritable or feel sick to your stomach.

Stop starving yourself, advises Ramsey. "Many people with anxiety disorders skip breakfast. I recommend that people eat things like eggs, which are a satiating and filling protein, and are nature's top source of choline. Low levels of choline are associated with increased anxiety." (Barnett, 2019)

Get Adequate Sleep

When the body is tired, it is unable to cope with stress and the symptoms of anxiety may be harder to manage. Make sure to make time for enough sleep every night. It may seem like a good idea to stay up to finish something, but then if you are unable to accomplish other tasks the next day because you are so tired, working late may have little overall benefit. Furthermore, it is dangerous to drive or operate machinery when we are tired.

If you are unable to get a good night's sleep, some people swear by taking naps. Some people do experience great stress release and other positive benefits from napping. Try it and see how it works for you. After a long, stressful or bad day at work, or when you feel you are in a high anxiety state, you may find it rejuvenating and calming to lay down and take a nap.

The desired result of the nap is that not only do you address some of the exhaustion you may feel from lack of sleep, but you may feel the relief of a calm body and brain. You may find a lot of peace in finding a quiet place to lay down your head for a few minutes or a few hours and then waking up to go on with your tasks.

Good Habits And Personal Traits

You could also develop some traits that help ensure your stress and anxiety is minimized. An example is making sure you are on time with everything, or that things are organized so that they can be accessed easily. You may develop the habit of planning carefully so that you are able to fit in all your activities. You may develop the habit of walking up the stairs instead of taking the elevator in order to fit in some exercise, or you might lay out your clothes the night before to avoid last-minute panic over choosing an outfit. You may get in the habit of making a batch of healthy snacks and lunches to put in the fridge so that you can grab them on the way out the door.

The Power Of The Right Tea

There are many people that swear by the calming and healthful powers of a good cup of the right tea. Hot herbal beverages have been used for centuries to calm the mind and the body.

Chamomile

Many people find a cup of camomile tea to be very relaxing, and some find it promotes good sleep. If you are feeling anxious, overwhelmed or jittery, a cup of chamomile tea might help to calm you.

Chamomile is also available as a nutritional supplement that contains apigenin as an active ingredient, along with dried chamomile flowers. A University of Pennsylvania Medical Center study found that patients with a generalized anxiety disorder (GAD) had a significant decrease in anxiety symptoms after taking chamomile supplements for eight weeks compared to patients that were given a placebo. (Perelman, n.d.)

Green Tea

Green tea contains antioxidants and an amino acid called L-theanine. L-theanine has been shown to help curb rising heart rates and blood pressure, and a few studies have found that it reduces anxiety. In a study, subjects with anxiety were given 200 milligrams of L-theanine before the test and those that took it reported that they were calmer and more focused during the test than those who did not take the L-theanine.

Although you can get L-theanine directly green tea, you would have to drink between five and 20 cups to get the same amount of L-theanine offered in a quality supplement. At that point, the impact of the caffeine may have a detrimental effect on your ability to be calm.

Herbal Supplements

Some herbal supplements are sedatives as well as having other health benefits, but this is not true of all of them. For example, L-theanine, as discussed above, may reduce the symptoms of anxiety, but it will not make you sleepy. Other herbal remedies have sedative effects that help calm us down and in many cases help us sleep. Good sleep has many positive health benefits including the minimization of anxiety symptoms. These sedative herbs should be used carefully. For example, do not take them when you need to be alert, drive or operate machinery. Barnett, 2015 discusses an assortment of herbal supplements which are summarized below

Hops

Most people associate hops with beer; however, the tranquilizing benefits of hops (*Humulus lupulus*) will not come just from drinking a beer. The actual sedative compound in hops is a volatile oil, so it is processed into extracts and tinctures. Hops is often used as a sedative and to promote sleep. "It's very bitter, so you don't see it in tea much unless combined with chamomile or mint," says Mark Blumenthal. (Barnett, 2015) It is sometimes also used in aromatherapy.

Note: Don't take sedative herbs if you are taking a prescription tranquilizer or sedative. Discuss with your doctor any supplements you are taking.

Valerian

Valerian (*Valeriana officinalis*) is a sedative that is used to treat insomnia. Due to its legitimate sedative compounds; it has been approved in Germany for treating sleep disorders.

Valerian is known to have a pungent, somewhat unpleasant smell, so it is often taken as a capsule or tincture, rather than as a tea. Valerian is often combined with other sedative herbs such as hops, chamomile, and lemon balm.

Lemon Balm

Lemon balm (*Melissa officinalis*) has been used since the Middle Ages to promote sleep and reduce the symptoms of anxiety. One study showed that lemon balm extracts of 600 mg were effective in producing a calming effect.

Lemon balm is very easy to grow, but it is usually sold as a tea, capsule or tincture. It may be combined with other herbs such as hops, chamomile, and valerian. Lemon balm should be used only in moderation because some studies have shown that high doses can increase the symptoms of anxiety. Always follow the directions on the product label and start with the smallest dose.

Passion flower

Passion flower is a natural herbal sedative that has been approved in Germany to treat nervous restlessness. It is also used to treat insomnia and reduce symptoms of anxiety. Some people have found it very effective. As with other sedatives, use it with caution.

Like other sedatives, it can cause drowsiness, so don't take it or other sedative herbs when you are also taking a prescription sedative or need to be alert.

Passion flower is recommended for short term use only. Don't take it for longer than one month at a time and never mix sedative herbs without medical advice.

Aromatherapy

There are many ways to use aromatherapy to treat symptoms of anxiety. Some of the scents are administered by deeply inhaling the scent from a small bottle that contains an oil or tincture. Sometimes, using a hand lotion with a calming scent can be a way to insert a regular soothing aromatherapy ritual into our day. Some people use potpourri or incense. Also, there are many diffuser products on the market today that release a mist into the air that is scented with whatever oil you put in it.

Lavender

Lavender (*Lavandula hybrida*) has been used as a calming scent for many centuries. The intoxicating aroma of lavender can bring us to a point of stillness and calm. Many people report feeling less anxious in environments scented with lavender oil. Many people carry lavender spray or oil to use periodically throughout the day when they feel the need to "chill".

Pine, Cedar And Aromatic Woods

A walk in the forest can be calming in part to the incredible smell of the trees and plants. It is possible to recreate these feelings by using an aromatherapy product or room scent that closely resembles the smell of a forest filled with evergreen coniferous trees.

Chapter Summary

In this chapter, you have learned about the various natural remedies that can be used to treat anxiety. There are many natural ways through which you can minimize and even eliminate the symptoms of anxiety. All of the natural remedies are rooted in the concept of self-care. When we neglect to take care of the basic needs of the body, it is not able to function effectively enough to withstand major stressors. Some of the major categories of self-care include exercise, proper nutrition and adequate sleep.

Some lifestyle changes and the development of good habits may assist to relieve stress by eliminating the sources of anxiety from your lives. Making time for exercise will have many positive benefits, including being an outlet for nervous energy, increasing the balance of hormones in our body, and keeping our body limber and fit. Being prepared for the day to come by preparing healthy meals and snacks that you can easily access and consume is an important part of ensuring good nutrition. Furthermore, making smart choices when you have to eat out is very important. Consuming healthy teas and enhancing the body's own ability to combat stress by taking nutritional supplements that promote relaxation and good sleep may be an option for you. Another option that many people find effective and pleasant is aromatherapy.

In the next chapter, you will learn about how to find peace and relieve anxiety through meditation...

CHAPTER NINE:

How to Meditate and Find Peace

Meditation is used throughout the world as a means to calm the mind and body and achieve a feeling of inner peace. Mediation has been used by Buddhists for this purpose for hundreds and maybe thousands of years. The modern practice of mediation has its roots in Asia and India, where the practice of meditation is widely spread and has evolved over the centuries to have unique cultural or religious characteristics. Despite any differences in words, actions, techniques or specifics of practice, all meditation has the same basic purpose. That purpose is to center the body, clear the mind and allow one to simply exist as an extension of the universe around you.

In today's modern world of the library and the internet, there are many ways to learn meditation techniques. There are some basic practices and beliefs that are common to most forms of meditation. Meditation requires you to train your mind and your body, and it may take time to master.

University of Wisconsin neuroscience lab director Richard J. Davidson, Ph.D. told *"The New York Times"* that in "Buddhist tradition, the word 'meditation' is equivalent to a word like 'sports' in the U.S. It's a family of activities, not a single thing," He goes on to explain that different meditation practices require different mental skills. (Gaiam, n.d)

Some people are able to meditate for hours. When you first start practicing meditation, it may be extremely difficult to sit for hours and think of nothing and have a clear, empty mind. Remember, don't beat yourself up! Don't be too hard on yourself! Focus on quality and not quantity. Make an effort to have really good but short sessions when you start and gradually increase the amount of time as you become better at controlling your mind and body.

If you enjoy nature, you may find it really helps you to center and focus yourself during a meditation session when you do it outside. The power of nature can fascinate and calm and be a path to relief from the stress you are under. Having the sounds of nature around you as you meditate can set a positive tone to your session. If you are not able to be outside surrounded by nature, you can use a nature soundtrack as the background music during your session. Some people believe that medication can only be done in silence, but that isn't true. It can be done in a loud crowded room, or with music on, or in any number of places with any number of background "soundtracks". This is because the focus of meditation is precisely about focus. Focus on both the specifics and the totality of the universe at the same time. When you are able to clear your mind no matter what distractions are around you, there is great peace and comfort to be experienced.

The Many Benefits of Meditation

Although relaxation may not always be the goal of meditation, it is often one of the beneficial results. After conducting research on people who practiced transcendental meditation in the 1970s, Herbert Benson, MD, a researcher at Harvard University Medical School, coined the phrase "relaxation response". He considered it "an opposite, involuntary response that causes a reduction in the activity of the sympathetic nervous system." (Gaiam, n.d)

The study of meditation has proved the following short-term benefits on the nervous system:

- Less anxiety
- Lower blood pressure
- Lower blood cortisol levels

- Improved blood circulation
- Lower heart rate
- Slower respiratory rate
- Greater feelings of well-being

In the Buddhist tradition of meditation, the ultimate benefit is the liberation of the mind's attachment to things it cannot control. This may include external stimuli, situations and circumstances, including strong emotions. By being able to free oneself of the fixation on desires or experiences, an "enlightened" practitioner is able to maintain a calm mind and develop a deep sense of inner harmony.

Concentration Meditation

The practice of concentration meditation requires the practitioner to focus on a single object or thought. This could involve focusing on your breathing, repeating a single word or mantra, staring at a candle flame, looking at a picture or item, listening to a repetitive gong, or counting beads on a mala. In this form of meditation, whenever your mind wanders, you simply refocus your awareness on the designated object. Rather than allowing random thoughts to permeate your full consciousness, you let them pass by and through your mind.

Remember, it is okay to only start with a few minutes at a time. It will get easier with practice.

Mindfulness Meditation

Mindfulness meditation is a bit different from concentration meditation. It encourages the practitioner to observe any and all thoughts as they drift through the mind. This observation is not meant to lead to consideration, evaluation or judgment of the thoughts, you are only meant to be aware of each thought as it comes up and passes through.

Through mindfulness meditation, you may notice patterns in your thoughts when you are anxious or calm. Finding stillness in this observation without judgment can give your thoughts and emotions a place to wander out of your anxious mind and out into the universe, where they will no longer impact you. With practice, you may find it helps you find a sense of inner peace.

Teresa M. Edenfield, a clinical psychologist in the Veterans Administration Medical Center in Durham, N.C., often uses mindfulness meditation to treat anxiety patients. "The act of practicing mindful awareness allows one to experience the true essence of each moment as it really occurs, rather than what is expected or feared," she says. (Barnett, 2019)

How do you begin the practice of mindful meditation? You start by simply "paying attention to the present moment, intentionally, with curiosity, and with an effort to attend non-judgmentally", Edenfield says.

Other Meditation Techniques

As mentioned previously, there are various other meditation techniques that are used around the world, and there is no one form that is right or wrong. Find the practice that works best for you. Some people use either concentration or mindfulness meditation. Some practitioners of meditation use a combination of meditation techniques. Most disciplines call for stillness but there are also forms of moving meditation such as tai chi, qigong, and walking meditation.

Simple Meditation For Beginners

There are many traditions of meditation. As a beginner, it can help to have a simple guide to some of the basic principles and practices of meditation. This meditation exercise has six steps and is an excellent introduction to meditation techniques.

Step 1: Sit Comfortably

Get seated in a comfortable position. You may have to try a few things before you are able to find a position that you can sit in for an extended period of time. If you sit on the floor, it is "traditional" to sit cross-legged, right leg over the left, right hand over the left hand, palms up, your right index finger gently touching your left thumb. Alternatively, place both hands on your lap comfortably. In all cases, keep your head up and your back straight. This sitting position is called the Peace Position or the meditation posture.

If you feel uncomfortable in this position, you may sit on a chair or sofa. Adjust your position until you feel completely comfortable. Ensure that you are in a position that will not restrict your blood circulation.

For those who are not able to sit up comfortably, it is also possible to meditate while lying down. Really you can meditate in any position, even standing up.

Gently close your eyes. Don't squeeze them shut tightly. Just drop your lids into a comfortable resting pose. Put a gentle smile on your face.

Step 2: Take Deep, Full Breaths

Next, take a deep breath. Hold it for 2 or 3 seconds and then exhale fully. Repeat inhaling and exhaling up to 10 times, and just breathe deeply in and out. Breathe in deeply until you feel the air pass through your lungs and reach the middle of your abdomen. Imagine that each cell in your body is fully taking in the feeling of happiness and joyfulness. Observe the way your body feels as it takes in air and lets it out. Some people swear by slowly breathing out through your nostrils, but others breathe out through their mouth with no truly detrimental impact on their positive experience. When you breathe out, consciously expel all your worries, stress, tension and negative feelings. Don't forget about what we learned earlier about deep breathing and apply it when you are meditating.

Step 3: Bring The Body And Mind To A Place Of Stillness

Take this time to just let go of all of your worries and anxieties. This is not the time or place to give them the stage in the theater of your consciousness. This is the time to stop thinking about the responsibilities of work, personal commitments to family or friends, or whatever else is making you anxious. Let your mind be relaxed and free from worry.

Keep breathing deep, full, regular breaths that feel natural and comfortable. Next, you should deliberately relax every muscle in your body. Start at the top of your head and make your way down to your toes.

When you are fully relaxed, try to maintain this state as long as you can. When your body is fully relaxed, it can more easily accept the sensations of lightness, joy and other positive energy that exist in our bodies or are available for us to experience.

Empty your mind and imagine you are sitting alone in a large open field. This space is peaceful where you have no attachments or problems. Then, imagine that your body is empty and hollow. Allow your body to feel lighter and lighter, as if it were becoming weightless, gradually melting away and becoming one with nature. What is left is your consciousness and a sense of oneness with the totality of the universe and the positive energy within it.

Step 4: Accept And Expand Upon This Feeling Of Peace And Calm

Next, focus on the center of your body about two finger widths above your navel. Simply concentrate on this area of your body with gentle sustained awareness, like a feather floating down from the sky to rest on a calm surface of a lake.

Imagine how soft and light the feather is when it touches the surface of the water. Imagine how soft and light you would feel if you were that feather. Hold onto the feeling of relaxation and keep your mind focused on the center of your body. Once you have centered your body, slowly and gently begin to imagine a neutral object that your mind can focus on so it does not wander. The moon, the sun, the flame of a candle, or the waves on a sandy beach are all good choices, but any object that makes you feel calm, peaceful and content will work.

Relax and simply picture the object resting in the middle of your peacefully resting body. It doesn't matter if you can picture it clearly. Think of your chosen object continuously, and don't let your mind wander.

Another way to focus the mind is to recite a short, soothing phrase. This is called a mantra. Recite the chosen word phrase softly in your mind and let the words resonate in the center of the object you envision in the center of your body. Keep your mind on the object and the phrase until your mind is still.

Step 5: Resist Outside Thoughts

Once your mind is completely still, you may just want to be still without your mind thinking about anything or even reciting your mantra. Once you have achieved stillness, it is okay to do that. If you lose your sense of meditative calm, simply back up a step and re-establish the use of the calming image and mantra until the feeling of peace and calm overcomes your body again.

Do not do anything beyond this. Let your mind be neutral to the thoughts that try to invade your carefully constructed sense of calm. Observe any new thoughts with a calm mind and remember to relax and let them pass through without judgment. Just keep observing and do not think of anything specific.

If you do this correctly, meditation will become easy and comfortable. Soon you will be able to get into this state effortlessly. Your mind will enter into a state of clarity, calm and contentment, and true inner knowledge may be revealed to you by your psyche.

Step 6: Send Your Positive Energy Out Into The World

Sharing positive energy with others spreads joy and compassion throughout the world, but we are not always in an emotional or physical state to be able to offer that to others. After meditation though, our minds and bodies are in a state of positivity that lends itself well to sharing.

The benefits of sharing kindness and other forms of positive energy include radiating a happy feeling from ourselves towards others and having it reflected back to us. We can share positive energy like love and kindness with the world by doing the following:

- Before ending your meditation session, when your mind is peaceful and still, you may find yourself filled with feelings of happiness. Focus your mind at the center of your body where you feel true love and good wishes. Then imagine condensing those good feelings into a bright sphere. Imagine this sphere or ball of love is effortlessly expanding in all directions away from your body, and then imagine it touching everyone in its path as it expands away from you.

Chapter Summary

You now have a firm handle on how to get started with the ancient practice of meditation. Use it to bring calmness and peace to your mind and body. Meditation has been proven over centuries to be an effective tool for managing anxiety and stress. Achieving stillness and a clear mind frees us from the negative outward expressions of our anxiety. Furthermore, meditation may have significant positive health benefits including lowering your blood pressure and improving blood circulation.

When you are preparing to meditate, there are some things that it might be helpful to prepare in advance. For example:

1. Select a comfortable and quiet place to sit in.
2. Select the item that you will use as your focusing object.
3. Choose a word phrase, or "mantra" to recite repeatedly to yourself, for example, "Clear and Bright" or "Beautiful World".

Summary of Meditation Steps

4. Assume the meditative posture of sitting comfortably with your hands at rest.
5. Relax your body and then your mind.
6. Become aware of and concentrate on a central area of the body, then imagine your focus object resting gently there.
7. Bring your body and mind to a point of calm, stillness and peace. Think of nothing, and if your mind becomes distracted, recite your mantra or picture your focus object.
8. Before getting up, make a conscious effort to spread your positive energy out from yourself to the entire world.
9. Get up carefully and slowly. Take some deep breaths and resume your day.

Now that you know how to meditate, you will be able to experience all the benefits it can bring to your life. Use it to calm yourself down and to clear your mind. You will find the calm you attain during meditation will seep over into the rest of your life.

In the next chapter, you will learn more about how to approach going to a therapist or other mental health professional...

CHAPTER TEN:

Tips for Going to A Therapist

In this book, we have focused on things that you can actively do to address your own personal battle with anxiety. As you learned, anxiety can include nervousness, self-doubt, worry, overthinking, and express itself in negative ways including nausea, sweating and panic attacks. By understanding your triggers and the underlying cause of your anxiety, it may be possible to interfere with its patterns, reduce your symptoms and find joy, peace and calm.

When the overwhelming and recurring symptoms of anxiety have a significantly negative impact on your life, it's time to get outside help. In Chapter 1 you learned about anxiety disorders such as PTSD, social anxiety disorder and generalized anxiety disorder, among others. Sometimes, despite our desire to manage our symptoms and underlying conditions on our own, we fail to achieve the results that we want. When this happens, or when you are in a state of overwhelming despair and are not able to cope with the negative impacts of anxiety on your mental and physical health, it is time to seek additional professional guidance to assist with the management of your condition.

Don't feel bad or beat yourself up for the fact that you need help. It's a sign of emotional maturity to recognize, seek and go through therapy. Mental health professionals may use a range of tools to assist you. There are many forms of therapy, but most commonly you will be offered some kind of talk therapy or medication, or both.

How Does Your Anxiety Express Itself?

It is important for every anxiety sufferer to understand the process involved in diagnosing a mental health condition. The underlying causes of your condition may be unique to you, and you may or may not understand what triggers your anxiety.

People show their anxiety in various ways. Some people become extremely talkative but they don't really make sense. They may be fixated on particular things. Other people become withdrawn and isolate themselves. Even individuals who usually seem outgoing can become fearful and withdrawn. All too often, a person's anxiety is caused by intrusive and obsessive thoughts. Therefore, that person may often feel confused or find it challenging to concentrate. Other people can feel restless and have a lot of nervous energy, while others may feel sick and depressed regularly. These are all major physical signs of anxiety. Other physical symptoms of anxiety may include tensed muscles as well as high blood pressure. Trembling and sweating can be common. Anxiety can cause digestive issues, difficulty in breathing, a racing heartbeat, insomnia or dizziness.

When your symptoms are something that you worry about, or if you are unable to manage your anxiety using the tools in this book, or if you are overwhelmed to the point of desperation, you should seek medical attention. Work with a professional to develop a treatment plan for your anxiety. Once you decide to get therapy, you will have to find and work with a mental health professional and get the most out of it that you can.

Tips About Working With A Therapist

Seeking therapy may seem mysterious. What will you discuss with the therapist? Are you capable of being honest? Is it possible to know if you are making progress? Prior to walking into the room, you need to be clear about your intention to seek help and be open to accepting it. Take some time to analyze your feelings and beliefs about therapists. If you have the belief that, "a head-shrinker is just going to talk about a bunch of emotional stuff, and that won't help me", then you are unlikely to open your mind up enough to accept the help that they offer. If you have difficulty interacting with others, group therapy may not be effective for you. You may need or want intensive individual counseling. You may be contemplating or need medication that helps to effectively manage your symptoms. You may need both medication to manage your symptoms and talk therapy to help you understand the underlying cause of your anxiety and what triggers your negative responses.

Choose Carefully

Once you have decided to seek professional help, you now face the challenge of finding a practitioner that you can work with. In some cases, as with prescribing psychiatrists, you may be referred to the only in your area or the only one that is currently taking patients. Work with whoever you are referred to and try to get the most out of the experience. Ask questions about their areas of practice and expertise, and how they typically handle cases like yours. Don't be afraid to get a second opinion, but also don't be afraid to take their advice and the medication that they prescribe to you. Do your research, however, and make sure that you are comfortable with what you learn about the medication they have prescribed, and that you feel safe working with them. See if there is any kind of feedback about their practice. Remember, a psychiatrist is usually focussed on prescribing medication, and may not practice any forms of therapeutic talk therapy at all.

When you are looking to work with a psychologist, you are likely to have more choices of practitioners. You may be able to get a referral, or you may have to research and select a practitioner yourself. It is important that you have a psychologist that you feel safe with and that you trust. You will be telling them your most personal secrets and you need to feel like they are on your side. Select a therapist carefully. Don't be afraid to speak to them on the phone and ask what their experience with counseling anxiety sufferers is. Ask them what kind of methods they use, or what type of practice they have. For example, are they followers of the Freudian methods or do they practice modern techniques such as cognitive behavioral therapy, tapping therapy, or art therapy? Do they typically work with people who have been through similar types of trauma as you have? Are they located somewhere that you can conveniently access? Do they have office hours that work with your schedule? Do they have fees that you can afford? If after your initial inquiries, you feel somewhat comfortable with what they can offer you, consider attending three sessions of therapy and see how you feel about it. It may take many sessions to make a lot of progress, but you may also find that you improve by leaps and bounds in a very short time. Everyone has a unique and personal experience with therapy, and it is meant to be tailored to your specific situation. Of course, because the therapist has likely worked with many others who also suffer from anxiety, they will be able to give you many useful insights about your condition and offer you viable ways to cope and manage on both a short-term and a long-term basis.

Schedule Your Sessions At The Perfect Time For You

Don't pick a time for your therapy that gives you extra stress. Schedule your appointments when you are capable of giving them your full attention. Specifically, you need to completely avoid scheduling your sessions when it is time to work or when you know that you will be pressed for time. If you are not very communicative in the mornings, and you have a lot of obligations during the day, a midday session may cause more harm than good. This is because these sessions can be very emotionally intense, and you may want to just go home and contemplate your session after you are done. If you are distracted by all the things you must still accomplish after the session, you may be excessively focussed on that, and not absorb all the insights of the session. On the other hand, the therapist may be able to give you useful short-term tools to help you get through the anxiety of that specific day. In these cases, you may not be focused on the overall underlying causes of your stress, but on coping strategies.

Whenever possible, consider giving yourself time and personal space in order to process and reflect upon your therapy.

Let It All Out In Therapy

Most people begin psychological therapy (talk therapy) by censoring themselves. It is difficult to be vulnerable, and we may not want to be judged. We may feel ashamed or embarrassed or angry about what we've been through. We may be afraid to relive our experiences in full. Be assured that therapy is meant to be a safe place. It is a safe place to talk about things you may have never told anyone. It is a safe place to cry. It is a safe place to ask questions about yourself and why you are the way you are.

Experts in the field encourage clients to say what they want and to not fear judgment. The role of the psychologist is to listen without judgment, help you come to terms with how you feel, and give you tools to improve your life. In doing so, you will be making progress every time you go to therapy.

Getting the most out of therapy does not mean you have to be on your best behavior or only talk about specific things. Getting the most out of therapy requires that you are authentic. You must believe that there will be a positive outcome if you talk about the things that have happened to you or that have been significant influences in your life. You must believe that the therapist will have ways to help you, or that just the act of releasing all of the emotion will help in itself. That way, your therapist can more effectively work on solutions that will help you to recover.

You Need to Be Orderly

The first thing you should do when booking a session is to check with the receptionist or administrator about how payment is handled. Make arrangements so that you don't have to pay on the way out when you are potentially in a rush, or in a vulnerable emotional state.

The next thing you need to consider is making a list of the urgent issues that you are facing. Remember making the list of all the things that cause you anxiety, or cause you to have anxious behaviors such as nervousness, invasive thoughts, and panic? If you didn't do it before, make that list now. If you have made the list, bring it with you when you go to talk to the therapist. You will be doing both of you a big favor, and it will increase the efficiency of your treatment process, as you will not be wasting time trying to figure out what your issues are. Having a good idea of what your symptoms are, and how your anxiety manifests itself gives the therapist "something to go on ". This may lead to the therapist asking you questions about the details of an event, or how it made you feel. They may ask you to divulge uncomfortable information about your experiences. This is all in an attempt to understand what the underlying causes and triggers of your anxiety are. Sometimes we may get angry or upset with our therapist for pushing us to an emotionally vulnerable place. You may feel that it isn't helping you because you don't see or feel any immediate relief from your symptoms. Don't be afraid to tell your therapist. They are used to these reactions and can explain the process to you and maybe even point out some of the improvements they have noticed in you that you may not have noticed yourself. Maybe you have a question regarding what you discussed in the last session. This is especially valuable to both you and the therapist because it means that you have been participating in your therapy outside of the sessions. Don't be afraid to ask them to explain something again or give you perspectives on what you might have been thinking or wondering about. Raise any concerns or questions at the onset of the next session. That way, you will have time to viably process the issues. In many cases, this will strengthen the alliance between you, as it indicates that you are actively engaged in your therapy. Some therapy takes time to work through, but it is valuable work, and you will reap many benefits in the end.

Stick to The Issues

It is critical to set boundaries for yourself and stick to the important issues during therapy. It may be difficult to "get right down to it", but this is what you are paying for. Resist the urge to make too much small talk or to merely go over the events in your life since the last appointment. Get right to business after saying your initial hellos and getting comfortable. Talk about what gave you anxiety since the last appointment. What triggered it and how did you feel? Did you cope better with it than last time? What have you been thinking about since your last appointment? If you are not sure what to say, let the therapist ask you questions and answer them honestly. If the questions upset you because they make you think of things that remind you of past trauma, that is okay. You are there to "unpack all your issues" and have the therapist "help sort them out".

Treat Therapy as A Collaboration

I'm sure it is now clear to you that therapy is an interactive process. It requires you to honestly share your memories and feelings with someone you may not have known at all before therapy started. You must rely on your therapist to help you, and the therapist must rely on you to come to your appointment and participate in a meaningful way so that they can help you. This collaboration is a give and take relationship that can give you great strength. This collaboration, when successful, will give you the confidence and tools that you need to address the sources of your anxiety and make changes in your life that allow you to manage the symptoms of your condition. Express yourself and your needs. Ask questions and read extra books or articles that may further your understanding of your condition.

Chapter Summary

Sometimes when we have anxiety we are able to control our symptoms on our own, using helpful techniques such as distraction, positive self-talk and meditation, among other things. Unfortunately, however, sometimes we are not able to fully cope with the stressors in our life, and we need professional help to understand our issues and develop effective coping mechanisms. When you notice that you are suffering from debilitating anxiety, you should see a therapist.

A psychiatrist and a psychologist are different, although some people are both. A psychiatrist will prescribe you medication, whereas a psychologist will talk to you about your problems and potential solutions. Some mental health issues, such as those caused by chemical imbalances in the brain require medication to be effectively treated. A proper diagnosis is important. Talk to the professional that you can get access to, and work with them to develop an understanding of your condition.

Make sure that if you are seeking medical help that you take a path that will not cause you extra anxiety. Make sure your appointments are scheduled at times when you are not super busy with other things before and after. Be honest with your medical care provider and tell them everything you can about what you know about your symptoms, triggers and underlying causes. As you talk about your life and your symptoms, your doctor will be able to form a diagnosis and help you develop tools to assist you in your daily life. Commit to honest, collaborative issues and stick to the issues. If you aren't sure what to say, let your therapist ask questions and answer honestly and fully. Get the most out of your sessions by practicing mindfulness and focusing entirely on the appointment. If you are distracted, tell your therapist why. It may be related to your condition and be a sign of a current anxiety reaction that they can help you with.

Making the decision to seek professional help is not always easy, but if you think you may need the advice of medical professionals, you probably do! At the very least, explore what therapy might be able to offer you. Go in with an open mind and a willingness to work with the therapist in an open and collaborative way. Many people benefit enormously from the help of a therapist. Maybe you will be one of them.

FINAL WORDS

In this book, you have learned about anxiety and how to stop it. Anxiety is a natural response to stress. When the mind and body are confronted with a stressor, the nervous system may be triggered to release adrenaline and cortisol, which can make us jittery and unable to handle stimuli. This is usually caused by the body's fear response that initiates the "freeze, fight or flight" behavior in us. The different impacts of stress may be expressed differently by various people. Anxiety may cause a rapid heartbeat, flashes of hot or cold, nervous behaviors, panic and gastrointestinal distress. Some people are able to manage stress and anxiety very well, but for others, it can have a debilitating effect on their lives.

Over the course of this book, we have reviewed everything you need to know about anxiety. You learned about what anxiety looks and feels like, and what the common symptoms are. In addition, we went over some of the major anxiety disorders that some people suffer from.

You have also learned a variety of tools and techniques to handle the symptoms of anxiety. When you are able to recognize the triggers for your anxiety, you can engage in positive self-talk, thought interruption and switching gears. Making a list of what you know about your anxiety helps you to understand what is happening to your mind and body. Also helpful in list form is all the things that bring you joy. Make a commitment to those things regularly. Making concerted efforts to incorporate joy into your life is very important to overcoming anxiety. The active pursuit of joy will increase the amount of happy hormones such as endorphins in your body and give you a positive experience that you can draw on later to rekindle feelings of contentment or joy.

For centuries, people have practiced various forms of meditation to help them calm their mind and body. Sit comfortably and clear your mind using focusing objects or a mantra. Meditation is an effective way to practice stillness and to bring peace and balance into your life.

Other natural remedies to anxiety include exercise, a nutritious diet, adequate sleep, and herbal supplements. Whether it be the practice of mindfulness and meditation, or the use of exercise and proper diet, there are many ways to influence how our body reacts to stress.

If you are experiencing debilitating anxiety and you find no relief from the techniques in this book, you may benefit from the assistance of professional mental health practitioners such as a psychiatrist or psychologist, or both. There is no shame in actively seeking out the help you may need.

Regardless of what method you use to reduce your nervousness and anxiety, the most important thing is that you are taking active steps towards managing your mental health, and that is a positive and healthy thing. Find ways to understand yourself better, recognize your triggers, and use this understanding, along with techniques for managing anxiety, to get your happiness back and find your inner peace.

RESOURCES

American Psychiatric Association & Parekh, Ranna, M.D, M.P.H. (2017) What Are Anxiety Disorders? https://www.psychiatry.org/patients-families/anxiety-disorders/what-are-anxiety-disorders. (accessed 2020).

Barnett, Robert A. (2019). 19 Natural Remedies for Anxiety. https://www.health.com/health/gallery/0,,20669377,00.html. (accessed 2020).

Brady, Krissy (2019) 13 Signs You're Sabotaging Your Own Progress in Therapy. https://www.huffingtonpost.ca/entry/signs-sabotaging-therapy-progress_l_5d40ac12e4b0db8affafb0a2. (accessed 2020).

Calmer You (2018) What To Do During An Anxiety Attack. https://www.calmer-you.com/anxiety-attack/. (accessed 2020).

Cooke, Justine (2016) Using Mindfulness to Overcome Anxiety. Visions Journal. https://www.heretohelp.bc.ca/visions/mindfulness-vol12/using-mindfulness-to-overcome-anxiety. (accessed 2010)

Daskal, Lolly (n.d.) 10 Simple Ways You Can Stop Yourself From Overthinking. https://www.inc.com/lolly-daskal/10-simple-ways-you-can-stop-yourself-from-overthinking.html. (accessed 2020).

Ferreira, Mandy (2017) 14 Mindfulness Tricks to Reduce Anxiety. https://www.healthline.com/health/mindfulness-tricks-to-reduce-anxiety#1. (accessed 2020).

Gaiam (n.d.) Meditation 101: Techniques, Benefits, and a Beginner's How-To. https://www.gaiam.com/blogs/discover/meditation-101-techniques-benefits-and-a-beginner-s-how-to. (accessed 2020).

Gottern, Ana (2018) 11 Ways to Stop a Panic Attack. https://www.healthline.com/health/how-to-stop-a-panic-attack#happy-place. (accessed 2020).

Headspace. (n.d.) Meditation for Anxiety. https://www.headspace.com/meditation/anxiety. (accessed 2020).

Henriques, Gregg, Ph.D. (2015) What is Mindfulness and How Does It Work? https://www.psychologytoday.com/ca/blog/theory-knowledge/201502/what-is-mindfulness-and-how-does-it-work. (accessed 2020).

Hofmann, Stefan G, Ph.D. (n.d) Facts about the effects of mindfulness. https://www.anxiety.org/can-mindfulness-help-reduce-anxiety. (accessed 2020).

Holland, Kimberly (2018) Everything You Need to Know About Anxiety. Healthline. https://www.healthline.com/health/anxiety. (accessed 2020).

Hovitz, Helaina (2018) Some Simple Ways to Turn Anxiety Into Excitement. https://greatist.com/live/how-to-turn-anxiety-into-excitement#3. (accessed 2020).

Jaworski, Margaret (n.d.) Living with Anxiety: How to Cope. https://www.psycom.net/living-with-anxiety/#anxiety-mind-andm. (accessed 2020).

Khuu, Cung (2018) How to Instantly Turn Anxiety into Excitement. https://medium.com/publishous/how-to-instantly-turn-anxiety-into-excitement-2c6c9495bc1. (accessed 2020).

Kind, Shelly (n.d.) Facts about the effects of mindfulness. https://www.anxiety.org/can-mindfulness-help-reduce-anxiety. (accessed 2020).

Li, Qing, Dr. (2018) Forest Bathing is Great for Your Health. Here's How to Do It. https://time.com/5259602/japanese-forest-bathing/. (accessed 2020).

Livni, Ephrat (2016) The Japanese practice of 'forest bathing' is scientifically proven to improve your health. https://qz.com/804022/health-benefits-japanese-forest-bathing/. (accessed 2020).

Matthews, Dan, CPRP (2020) 15 Ways to Stop Overthinking and Worrying About Everything. https://www.lifehack.org/articles/communication/how-to-stop-overthinking-everything.html. (accessed 2020).

Mayo Clinic, Anxiety Disorders. https://www.mayoclinic.org/diseases-conditions/anxiety/symptoms-causes/syc-20350961. (accessed 2020).

Mays, Mitchell, Dr. (Mindful Staff (2019) How to Meditate. https://www.mindful.org/how-to-meditate/. (accessed 2020).

Moffitt, Debra (n.d.) Nine Simple Practices to Embrace Joy. https://www.beliefnet.com/wellness/personal-growth/nine-simple-practices-to-embrace-joy.aspx. (accessed 2020).

Perelman School of Medicine (n.d.) Generalized Anxiety Disorder. https://www.med.upenn.edu/ctsa/general_anxiety_symptoms.html. (accessed 2020).

Risher, Brittany (2018) This Is When to See a Mental Health Professional About Your Anxiety. https://www.self.com/story/when-to-see-professional-anxiety. (accessed 2020).

Roselle, Tom, Dr. (2017) 19 Natural Remedies for Anxiety. https://www.drtomroselle.com/19-natural-remedies-anxiety/. (accessed 2020).

Spiritual Progress Guide Admin (2015) Meditation for Inner Peace. http://spiritualprogressguide.com/blog-post/meditation-for-inner-peace. (accessed 2020).

Tartakovsky, Margarita, M.S. (2018) Therapists Spill: 10 Tips for Making the Most of Therapy. https://psychcentral.com/lib/therapists-spill-10-tips-for-making-the-most-of-therapy/. (accessed 2020).

U.S. Department of Health and Human Services (n.d) What are the five major types of anxiety disorders? https://www.hhs.gov/answers/mental-health-and-substance-abuse/what-are-the-five-major-types-of-anxiety-disorders/index.html. (accessed 2020).

Wehrenberg (2005) 10 Best-Ever Anxiety-Management Techniques. https://www.psychotherapynetworker.org/magazine/article/774/10-best-ever-anxiety-management-techniques. (accessed 2020).

Werner, Carly (2019) I'm Afraid of the Future. How Can I Enjoy the Present? https://www.healthline.com/health/fear-of-the-future#1. (accessed 2020).

Wikipedia (2020) Jon Kabat-Zinn. https://en.wikipedia.org/wiki/Jon_Kabat-Zinn. (accessed 2020).

YOUR FREE GIFT

Thank you again for purchasing this book. As an additional thank you, you will receive an e-book, as a gift, and completely free.

This guide gives you 14 Days of Mindfulness and sets you on a two-week course to staying present and relaxed. Practice each of the daily prompts to learn more about mindfulness, and add it to your daily routine and meditations.

You can get the bonus booklet as follows:

To access the secret download page, open a browser window on your computer or smartphone and enter: **bonus.derickhowell.com**

You will be automatically directed to the download page.

Please note that this bonus booklet may be only available for download for a limited time.

Printed in Great Britain
by Amazon